"Melissa Wood is a genuine person ṇ ... urge you to read this book, because it captures some of the essence of who she is. Fear is one of the biggest problems we have in life, and it clogs the brain and prevents us from seeing God's truth. This book will help you achieve a lifestyle of freedom!"

—**Jeffery Barsch**, Author of *Educational Sozo* and *Praying for the Brain*, Director of Praying for the Brain Ministries

"Countless individuals are emotionally and relationally crippled by fear and anxiety. Religious fear is quite literally the clinical cause of numerous psychological and mental health issues – not to mention the fundamentalist extremism and terrorism of our time. While I strongly adhere to 'the fear of the Lord' in the sacred texts, unfortunately our own twisted human concepts have been projected onto these scriptures. We must take the final word on the matter which is that 'perfect love casts out all fear' (1 John 4:18). All men crave to 'fear' something – in that we long for something outside our control. Hence we go bungee jumping, ride roller coasters, watch Texas Chainsaw Massacre and do our own taxes. And God is truly untamed and outside of our control. But the fear of the Lord is not at all related to our earthly slavish definition of anxiety. It is the only true fear that intoxicates us and is capable of 'delighting in' (Isaiah 11:3). We do not "fear God" because he is brutal, moody, schizophrenic or angry. We 'fear God' because he is a billion volts of beauty, gladness, happiness and sweetness - and we are just a two-volt fuse! We cannot handle the intensity of this love!

"In the following book allow yourself to experience the liberty of pure divine love as Melissa Joy Wood explores the truth in great depth that 'there is no fear in love.'"

—**John Crowder**, Sons of Thunder Ministries & Publications, www.thenewmystics.com

"Melissa Wood's insightful and inspiring book begins with the premise that any area of our lives that doesn't glisten with the love of God is under the influence of fear—cowering, debilitating fear. Her exploration of the true meaning of 'the fear of the Lord' challenges centuries of misunderstanding and will shake your understanding of Father God's heart toward you to your core. Jesus, the perfect revelation of the Father, said if we live in accordance with His teachings we will be His true disciples and know the truth that makes us free. In Eliminating Fear, Melissa marks the path to living in the freedom Jesus promises."

—**Dennis Ricci**, Author/Speaker and Director of
Conejo Valley Healing Rooms

"This book will inspire you to approach your life and ministry from a new perspective. I'm honored to know and watch Melissa advance freedom in this present move of God. Her Biblical truth and life ex-perience will keep you captivated as you read this book. She carries a rich inheritance and wisdom beyond her years. I proudly endorse this book. Enjoy the read…You will blessed and stretched!"

—**Wendell McGowan**, Author of *Firewalker* and *The Unfolding*,
Director of Wendell McGowan Ministries

Eliminating Fear

The Destiny Hub Press
415 Pearson Rd., Port Hueneme CA 93041
World Wide Web: www.thedestinyhub.com
E-mail: info@thedestinyhub.com

The Destiny Hub Press is the book publishing division of The Destiny Hub, Inc., a network of faith-based ministers, pastors, and leaders whose goal is community transformation. For more information about local and regional activities, write The Destiny Hub, Inc., 415 Pearson Rd., Port Hueneme CA 93041, or visit The Destiny Hub website at www.thedestinyhub.com.

All Scripture quotations, unless otherwise indicated, are taken from THE HOLY BIBLE, ENGLISH STANDARD VERSION®, ESV® Copyright © 2001, 2007, 2011 by Crossway Bibles. All rights reserved worldwide.

Images of water crystals used with permission from Hiro Emoto, Office of Masaru Emoto, LLC.

Editor: Monica Faulkner, Faulkner Editorial Services, Los Angeles CA, www.monicafaulkner.com
Cover Design: Aaron Ford, DigiCom Designs, Oxnard, CA, www.digicomdesign.com

ISBN 978-0-9862910-0-5

ACKNOWLEDGEMENTS

To my husband, Rick, who has faithfully walked me through the phases of finding freedom in my life. Thank you for your endless love and boundless mercy. I love you.

To my kids, Abigail, Brennan, and Caleb for being patient with Mommy through days and nights of writing and processing. Your love has strengthened me.

To my parents, Linda Murphrey and John Murphrey, for developing who I am today. Thank you for valuing my goals and dreams, and thank you for cheering me on through everything.

To Steve Gorrell, for being one of the greatest supporters of this book that I have had. Thank you for being a beautiful demonstration of how to face death without fear. You have inspired the way I live. You will be missed.

To my friends and church family, for giving me the life lessons and opportunities for growth I have needed. Thank you for your forgiveness, grace, and encouragement. You have taught me over and over again about eliminating fear in my relationship with God. I am indebted to many of you.

To my editor, Monica Faulkner, for hearing my voice and helping me articulate it in the best way possible. Thank you for helping to shine a light on my message and teaching me so much in the process.

FOREWORD

"Fear is the thief of dreams."
—Brian Khans

How our fears limit us! We all have them—little fears, big fears, subtle or overt—based on real life or only imaginary. However they begin, fears that endure become part of our every day thinking, like an old broken chair in the house of our mind that has been in the wrong place so long we simply fail to see it and automatically alter our course. Though occasionally we stub our toe on the useless obstruction, it has been there so long, we never think of just removing it.

How would we live if we had no fear? How much hope could we host? Fears can become the borders of expectations. We accept their limits, like an invisible fence between us and joy.

"I am an old man and have known a great many troubles, but most of them never happened."
—Mark Twain

Whether based in reality or simply a lie we adopted, the effect of fear is the same. A fear does not have to have ever been real in order to limit us.

This book deals head on with the lynchpin of fear—the fear of God. Though particularly powerful, it is a fear that simply is not real. There is nothing more damaging than trying to include fear in any relationship, especially our most intimate and life giving relationship with Father, Son and Holy Spirit.

We become what we behold. Do we behold the Father of Jesus with a single face of love or two faces? Is God Love plus fear or only perfect love? Does God have conflicting feelings about you or simply love you because He begat you?

"Love is what we were born with. Fear is what we learned here."
—Marianne Williamson

We have heard that God wants us to "balance" His love with some special kind of fear. However, as the author guides us to see, this cannot possibly be true. Fear is torment and God is not its author!

"There is no fear in love; but perfect love casteth out fear: because fear hath torment. He that feareth is not made perfect in love." (1 John 4:18, King James Version)

In this compelling book we taste and see that His justice is completely satisfied that mercy triumphs. Here we see His love without condition is so much bigger and more joyful than we have heard! Join us on a journey to clarity and freedom as we embrace the powerful and single-minded perfect love of God that casts out fear!

—**Rod Williams**, Senior Leader of Kainos Church, Santa Cruz, California

PREFACE

None of us is untouched by fear. Many of us are trapped by it. If we are honest with ourselves, any area of our life that is not glistening with love is under the influence of fear.

Fear is not our friend. It does not protect us. It does not help us make good decisions. The commonly accepted belief that fear can be used as a positive motivator in our lives is a grand deception. Once we fall prey to it, the emotional dying process begins.

> Fear comes in many sizes and shapes. At one end of the fear spectrum is the megalomaniac—the type of fear demonstrated by Hitler, Stalin, Castro and other despots. Their rise to power was fueled by fear: fear of the Jews, Gypsies, Slavs, Christians, capitalism, and freedom itself. Such thugs of history were consumed with fear, but rather than eradicate it, they embraced it, joined their hearts to it and became one with it. Fear became their weapon against society, splitting, dividing, conquering, and destroying. These ambassadors of evil, with hearts and minds so shaped by anti-love, created mangled societies battered by fear. And history is clear: where fear abounds, death quickly follows.
>
> On the other end of the spectrum from the megalomaniac is the human "mouse." Afraid of rejection, fearful of embarrassment, terrified of criticism, people made meek by fear abase them-

selves into doormats walked on by the entire world. They never say no, never stand up, and never set boundaries because they are controlled by fear of what others might say or how others might respond or think.

In-between these two extremes exist all manner of fear-ridden apparitions morphing insecurity into their own unique survival mechanism—the playground bully, the proud, the arrogant, the racist, the bigoted and the sexist. Here you'll also find the alcoholic, the drug addict, sex addict and shopaholic; the religionist, cultist and separatist; the philanderer, the liar, the cheater and fraud—each motivated by fear, each seeking some way to protect self, promote self or advance self. But rather than surviving, rather than healing, rather than growing, all are slowly dying and destroying others in the process. Life, health and happiness are only found where love flows free. And love only flows free where the truth about God is known![1]

I wrote this book to renew our minds…to change the way we think. Mind renewal is one of my passions. For years, I have watched people in church, ministry school, counseling, and relationships have their entire lives restored when their minds were renewed to the truth of who God is and how much He loves them. Fear is the enemy of that truth. Fear is the ultimate liar, and it's time to uncover it for what it is. It's time to reverse the lies, redeem the stolen, and recover the lost. It's time for Love to take center stage and for Faith to fill our minds.

---

[1] Timothy R. Jennings, M.D., *The God-Shaped Brain*, (Downers Grove, IL: InterVarsity Press, 2013), 46-47.

God is good. Fear is not. Let's watch the two collide in the pages ahead.

CHAPTER ONE

"I Have a Fear Of...":
Facing Our Personal Fears

The enemy is fear. We think it's hate, but it's actually fear.
Mohandas K. Gandhi

Fear has been my struggle. It has also been where I have found my greatest victory. Here is where the tools for eliminating fear begin to be revealed. We start by focusing on the positive outcome of facing our fears. Victory over fear begins with focusing on what I am *not* afraid of to help me overcome what I fear.

My struggle with fear began early. From my infancy until I was four years old, I lived in a bedroom with train-themed wallpaper. Everywhere my eyes turned, there were trains. During the years I spent in this bedroom, I was dealing with many physical disabilities. I had been born with a severe clubfoot that required surgeries and movement-limiting leg casts. As I lay in my crib, barely able to move, surrounded by trains, the nightmares began. Night after night I would dream about trains coming after me. Over and over again I would wake up afraid. I was usually trapped in a cast, so I would suffer through the fear without anyone being able to comfort me. My parents could only comfort me a little, because I was encased in a cast.

As I got older, the irrational fears increased, causing many physical and emotional disorders. Though many of these fears were irrational, I did face some scary things in my childhood. Aside from the clubfoot, I had chronic pneumonia through age eight and was hospitalized many times for that. I developed megacolon at age nine and spent a three-month stint in the hospital, during which I could not eat or drink, and I was fed through a tube in my nose. I also experienced a lot of family trauma: the divorce of my parents, feelings of abandonment, and other things common to many. Fear became my safe place. Fear made me feel in control even if my life was out of control. If I felt fear, then it communicated to me to put up emotional walls. When my walls were up, I could stay safe. It was a subtle yet destructive lie. Throughout this book, I want to address fear and its many deceptive faces. I don't believe that any measure of fear should be allowed influence in our lives—and at the end of this book, I believe you will find freedom from this nasty foe named "fear."

Focusing on the Positive

Let me repeat a statement I made in the first paragraph of this chapter:

Victory over fear begins with focusing on what I am not afraid of to help me overcome what I fear.

For example, here's a list of things I've been afraid of:

- I was afraid of abandonment.
- I was afraid of the freeway overpass crushing me.
- I was afraid of my child being in a car accident.
- I was afraid of being in a plane crash.
- I was afraid of enclosed spaces.

- I was afraid of being lied to.
- I was afraid of a tsunami taking over my home and family.
- I was afraid of....

Focusing on the list of my fears makes me feel defeated and over-whelmed. Instead, I start with focusing on things I am not afraid of:

- I am not afraid of public speaking.
- I am not afraid of what people think about me.
- I am not afraid of failure.
- I am not afraid of risking new things.
- I am not afraid of starting new businesses.
- I am not afraid of intimacy with my spouse.
- I am not afraid of what you think about this book.
- I am not afraid of God.
- I am not afraid of carrying a few extra pounds.
- I am not afraid of people who disagree with me.
- I am not afraid of living by a schedule.
- I am not afraid of serving someone else.
- I am not afraid of honesty.
- I am not afraid of confrontation.
- I am not afraid of being misunderstood.
- I am not afraid of life.
- I am not afraid.

Do you feel the difference? Do you feel the power rising up in the declaration of these positive statements? Do you see that the simple focus on the positive creates an increase of faith, even if only for a minute?

My "I am not afraid of" statements are things I am truly *not* afraid of. When focusing on those things, the things I *am* afraid of feel much smaller. Now what if I made "I am not afraid of" statements about the things I actually am afraid of?

- I am not afraid of abandonment.
- I am not afraid of unexpected tragedy.
- I am not afraid for my child's life.
- I am not afraid of enclosed spaces.
- I am not afraid of being lied to.
- I am not afraid of a tsunami, earthquake, or any natural disaster.
- I am not afraid.

This may sound fake to you. You may think I'm allowing myself to live in deception or in a false reality. I want to argue the contrary. My faith took a step forward with these positive declarations. The reason my faith took a small step forward is because faith comes by hearing: "So faith comes from hearing, and hearing through the word of Christ." (Romans 10:17, English Standard Version).

You are not lying when you speak out loud the beliefs and emotions you desire to uphold and express. Why? Because God, Who is with you, is not afraid. He has given you complete ability for anything that is possible with Him. Declare Who He is, what He believes, and what He can do—because with Him, it is true for you as well. This is not about trying to "make" something happen. This is awakening your faith to truth by hearing it.

There are two excellent Old Testament illustrations in the Bible of declaring beliefs and emotions this way. The first is God's instruction to Israel to walk into times of adversity with strength because He has given them victory regardless of the overwhelming appearance of their enemies. In Joel 3:10b, God says, "Let the weak say, 'I am a warrior.'" This is not wishful thinking.

This is the Israelites calling forth who they are—with God on their side.

The second illustration is the story of Gideon in Judges 6-8. Gideon hid himself in a wine press in fear of his life, because a massive army was rising up against his people. He felt he was a coward and a failure, incapable of anything great. An angel appeared and called out to Gideon, "The Lord is with you, O Mighty Man of Valor." What? Who? Gideon? The frightened one hiding from the world in a wine press? A warrior? Yes. That's how God saw him. When the truth of who God said Gideon was became the focus, Gideon was able to come out and face what was ahead. God knows the potential in you—in each one of us. He also knows the limitless possibilities and infinite power we all possess in and through Him. The one positive statement about Gideon launched him on a journey of small steps of faith and trust that brought a lifetime of victory into his destiny.

What Is Possible with God

My first experience of realizing that so much more was possible was when I underwent a radical shift in my beliefs in 2004. As I briefly mentioned before, I was diagnosed at age nine with a very rare disorder called megacolon, caused by the stress I internalized as a child. After a series of difficult events—family drama, bankruptcy and foreclosure of our home, moving schools repeatedly, etc.—I suddenly stopped having bowel movements. The cilia in my large intestines, the small fibers that push digested food through the colon, completely shut down. I went three weeks without having a bowel movement before my parents realized something was seriously wrong. Because I was so compacted, I would eat and then vomit. It was more dangerous to my health than my parents and the doctors realized. My parents took me to ten or eleven doctors with no successful diagnosis. No one understood what was wrong with me. I had all the uncomfortable tests you can imagine done for my colon and some that had nothing to do with my colon.

Finally we found a wonderful gastroenterologist who discovered the issue: megacolon. Because my cilia had shut down and nothing was moving through my colon, it had stretched so much that the muscles became dysfunctional. My colon had stretched to almost six times its normal size. I looked like a nine-year-old who was five months pregnant.

At this point, I was hospitalized for almost ninety days. Many methods were used to try and bring me back to health. I was given betadine enemas, forced to drink gallons of laxative liquids, and eventually fed through a tube in my nose in order to avoid the colon completely. I did come back to place of physical health, but not to a place of healing.

When I left the hospital, I had turned ten. I still didn't have a functioning colon. So between the ages of ten and nineteen, I would go five days at a time without having a bowel movement. Evacuating my bowels meant making strong laxative teas with high doses of senna that I took once every five days. I would stay home from school or weekend activities every fifth day to be near a bathroom as the raw senna flushed my system, a process accompanied by extreme pain and cramping. From the time I was ten until I turned nineteen, I never had a bowel movement on my own between those fifth-day cleansings. As a child, it was a difficult and embarrassing way to live.

When I was nineteen, I went to see an internal medicine doctor who re-ran all the tests I'd had many years before. He said that the laxatives and the senna were turning the inside of my colon black, and that I had to find a natural way to stay cleaned out, or I was destined to have a complete colostomy by the age of thirty. I began giving myself water/salt enemas every single day. Sometimes I would try to go a couple of days without one to see if I could have a bowel movement on my own, but I was always disappointed because there was no change in my colon. I gave myself daily enemas until I was twenty-four.

Then everything changed.

I used to pray about my megacolon. I was raised to believe that healing was not all that common or that it only happened "on the mission field." So I did not even know if my prayers for God to heal me were heard or if healing was even a possibility. But I was desperate, so that was what I prayed for—healing.

In March 2004, Ron Fisher, a friend of my husband, Rick, and mine from California, came to visit us and our two children. In the church where Ron was working, they were experiencing great miracles of God, including people being miraculously healed. I asked him to pray for me. He began to pray for the emotional issues that had started in my childhood—the stressors that had caused my megacolon. I did not tell him about these things, but he seemed to know. I did not receive a physical healing that day, but I did have two amazing things occur: a measure of deep, emotional healing, and an inner confirmation and new-found belief that I *would* experience the healing of my megacolon.

Through an interesting course of events, three months later, our family moved to Port Hueneme, California, to attend The Church at Parkview, where Ron was working. We had no job and no home, just a strong feeling from God that we should go. We arrived on June 4, 2004. On Tuesday evening, June 7, 2004, Rick and I attended a small prayer meeting of six people. These six people did not know me at all. The pastor, Terry Westerman, was there also. It was the first time I had met him. I took a risk that night by telling them about my megacolon and that I wanted to be healed. This precious group of people began to pray and lay hands on me, and I immediately felt overcome. Terry began praying about the exact symptoms, which I hadn't told him about. He began praying about the cilia and the other functions of my colon as if he knew me. I could feel God through him. After an extended time of prayer during which I slipped into a state of semi-consciousness on the pew, the prayer meeting ended with Terry declaring God would give me a sign that I could physically feel that night as confirmation of my healing.

I went back to Ron's home, where we were staying, and minutes later began experiencing intense pain. I wasn't sure what was happening, but I was experiencing something inside me physically. The pain eventually passed and I went to sleep that night without a bowel movement.

The following morning began with my asking everyone in the house, "What does it feel like when you need to poop?" because I needed to know what it felt like to have a natural bowel movement impulse. Why? I could feel pressure and something different—something I had not experienced in fifteen years. What happened next? I had a bowel movement! No laxatives, no enemas—nothing but me and the power of God coursing through my colon. I had experienced a miracle of healing. Not only was healing still possible, but it happened to me. I still live in my complete and full healing today.

My healing marked a definitive change in my life and in Rick's as well. Something we had thought was impossible had happened to us. What else was possible? What else could our God do? We didn't know at that moment, but we chose to begin to trust that there was more. Our language started changing. Our beliefs were not quite there, but what we were now saying was possible began to have an impact on our deep-seated beliefs.

As I've been telling this story, I've repeatedly used the phrase "my megacolon." How many times do we do this in our lives—empower fear, sickness, and hopelessness by our very own words? We believe that our identity is somehow defined by the difficulties we are facing. But it was never "my" megacolon. It was just megacolon that happened to be wreaking havoc in my life. That megacolon was not meant for me. It was not God's desire to see me in pain and unable to function.

You may ask, "What about the pain, sickness, and suffering all around the world? Are you saying it is people's own fault that they're experiencing those things?" Honestly, I can only reveal to you what revelation I've had thus far, nothing more. I do not know the answers to all of your questions, but I do know that what I believe about God is directly related to what I will see manifested in my life. What I believe about God is also directly formed by what I say about Him, what I say about myself, and what I say about my life. I love what Dan McCollum, Director of the School of Worship at Mission Church in Vacaville, California, says, "Your experience will always rise to your level of declaration."

Declarations Shape Our Reality

Declarations are the foundation of what I am pointing to in this chapter. A declaration is something you say or speak over your life. As Proverbs 18:21 states, declarations and affirmations can be positive or negative: "Life and death are in the power of the tongue, and those who love it will eat its fruit."

The words that roll off our tongues have the power to shape our circumstances. The words we hear ourselves say impact what we believe. And what we believe affects how we live our lives. When we use words out loud or to ourselves, what are we saying? What are we declaring?

A positive declaration is similar to a positive affirmation. As I mentioned at the beginning of the chapter, I declare "I am not afraid of tragedy" instead of affirming the opposite. Developing declarations to combat areas of fear in our lives is highly effective, and it has been one of the most powerful tools I've used in battling megacolon.

What does my history of megacolon have to do with fear? Everything. Every fear in life that you have was created by a belief that you hold. Let me share some of the negative beliefs I've faced:

- I did not believe that God could do a better job with my life than I could, so I pushed and overextended myself out of fear that I might not fulfill my destiny.

- I did not believe that God was protecting me, so I protected myself by trying to control others.

- I did not believe that anyone was trustworthy, so I assumed that most people were lying.

- I did not believe that I had power over my environment, so I allowed my emotions to become my compass.

These debilitating beliefs shaped the fears that shaped my actions. Fear may masquerade as wisdom, thoughtfulness, or peace of mind; but in reality it is only a deceptive perversion of those positive qualities. Fear tries to tell us that it's just "healthy fear" (which is addressed in the next chapter) and that its job is to keep us safe. It may seem to do so in the moment—but in the long run, our lives will be short-changed.

The Shape of Our Beliefs

Our experiences also shape what we believe. Whether it's how we were raised, what we were told, how we've been treated, or where we've lived, our experiences have shaped much of our thinking. But here's a news flash: Experience does not equal truth.

- Because someone in your neighborhood was shot does not mean your child will be.

- Because you were cheated on does not mean it will happen again.

- Because your aunt died of cancer does not mean that you will.

- Because you grew up with an abusive mother does not mean that all women are untrustworthy.

- Because you grew up with a distant father does not mean that all men do not know how to express love.

Our beliefs and thinking that were shaped by our experiences and developed throughout our lives can actually begin in the womb. According to Christian psychiatrist Timothy R. Jennings, MD:

> One possible avenue for anxiety to be instigated is a pre-birth effect on the brain. Brain development begins in utero. Unfortunately, since any unusually high stress causes the body to release stress hormones (glucocorticoids), if this occurs during a woman's pregnancy, those stress hormones cross the placental barrier and alter the developing fetal brain. ...Which means that a child born to a high-stress mother will have a brain less capable of calming itself and turning off alarm circuitry.[1]

---

[1] Timothy R. Jennings, M.D., *The God-Shaped Brain*, (Downers Grove, IL: InterVarsity Press, 2013), 48-49.

Fortunately, though, the way we choose to exercise our brain today can reshape its circuitry today. As our belief systems change, our brain circuitry can be reshaped. God still works miracles, and He invites us to join in on the process. As Dr. Jennings notes:

> The good news is that many brain regions remain changeable throughout life, thanks to a condition called neuroplasticity. This is particularly true of the prefrontal cortex. As we exercise healthy neural circuits, these circuits develop, strengthen and expand. Conversely, the brain prunes unhealthy circuits when we leave them idle.[2]

This is wonderful news. Many brain regions remain changeable throughout life, particularly the prefrontal cortex. It's our "motherboard"—all of our decision-making lies in our prefrontal cortex. I say it's time for us to reprogram our motherboard. God has given me the power to create new circuits of thinking and believing inside my brain, which means I no longer have to blame people in my life or circumstances around me. I can take charge of how I think, which will affect how I feel, which will in turn affect how I live.

Tony Robbins, a popular motivational speaker, says that we need to move from focusing on our resources to our resourcefulness. Many of us blame the resources that we've been dealt: people, finances, job, home, childhood, etc. What if we instead took note of the resourcefulness that lives inside each one of us and gives us the power to change things? The living God, Who lives in me, can do the impossible. He has created me with hope and faith, and those gifts can change how I view life. I have the

---

[2] Timothy R. Jennings, M.D., *The God-Shaped Brain*, (Downers Grove, IL: InterVarsity Press, 2013), 56.

power to align my beliefs with His, and that will create forward motion in my life.

If we allowed every negative experience in our lives to develop into a belief about how we should live, our lives would be stunted. Many of us might never dare to ride a bike because of the fear of falling. Inventions could stay hidden because of the fear of failure. Isolation might be chosen because of the fear of rejection. Life would be miserable because basic life choices would be based on fear.

So if experience doesn't equal truth, why do we allow some of our beliefs to be based on experience alone? For example, my family line is riddled with instances of adultery. I've witnessed some of this adultery myself and have even been its victim. These experiences could have easily shaped many of my beliefs about love and relationships. I could have come to believe that spouses will never be faithful, that marriage beds will never be honored, that infidelity is inevitable, etc. I have direct evidence and experience for these beliefs. The problem is, as soon as I decide to agree with these fears and allow any of them become beliefs in my life, I've thrown hope out of the window.

The Effects of Hope on Fear

The substance of the faith that replaces fear is the assurance of what we hope for. The dictionary states that hope is the "desire accompanied by expectation of or belief in fulfillment (noun)" or "to desire with expectation of obtainment (verb)."[3]

This aligns well with Proverbs 13:12, "Hope deferred makes the heart sick, but a desire fulfilled is a tree of life." I like to define hope as the fuel to my engine of faith. It keeps my beliefs going

---

[3] http://www.merriam-webster.com/dictionary/hope.

upward. It provides a way out of the most discouraging of situations.

Here are some additional verses on hope:

> "For in this hope we were saved. Now hope that is seen is not hope. For who hopes for what he sees? But if we hope for what we do not see, we wait for it with patience." (Romans 8:24-25)

> "May the God of hope fill you with all joy and peace in believing, so that by the power of the Holy Spirit you may abound in hope." (Romans 15:13)

And the most powerful verse:

> "Now faith is the assurance of things hoped for, the conviction of things not seen." (Hebrews 11:1)

According to scientific research, hope is why the "placebo effect" works on patients. A placebo is a substance with no known medical effects, such as sterile water, saline solution, or a sugar pill. The placebo effect refers to the phenomenon in which some people experience some type of benefit after the administration of a placebo. In short, a placebo is a fake treatment that in some cases can produce a very real response. Why does this work? Because the patient is expecting—hoping for—a certain outcome. Hope and positive expectations play an important role in the placebo effect, because the more strongly patients hope and expect the treatment to work, the more likely they are to exhibit a placebo response.

My expectation lies in the hope of a God Who comes through for me in every circumstance and removes all fear. Fortunately, this God is not a placebo. He truly is the God Who comes through for me, the God Who heals me, the God Who protects me, and the God Who loves me. Steve Backlund, Director of Igniting Hope Ministries, says, "I know I am making progress in renewing my mind, because my hope is rising."

Let's recap:

- Our experiences shape our beliefs, and our beliefs shape our actions.
- New beliefs can be shaped by what we declare.
- Our new beliefs can reshape our brains, which will change the way we think, feel, and live.

It is the power of declaration that invites you to create change within your mind. This begs the question: "What do I declare?"

The answer lies in another question: "What does God say?" This may sound oversimplified, but what God says about any area of your life is a truth you can believe. What God says is of the utmost importance. For there to be any change in our lives, it's vitally important that we find out what God is saying. You will hear the theme of "what God is saying" over and over again throughout the pages of this book.

The Voice of God vs. the Voice of Fear

One of my passions is for people to learn to hear the voice of God in their everyday lives, because He is always speaking. His words did not end with the last page of the Bible. More than anything, the Bible is God's opportunity for us to become familiar with how He works and speaks. The Bible shows us repeatedly that God wants to talk to us. He developed unique and individual ways to speak to each person in the Bible.

In fact, He never spoke the same way twice. There was only one recorded burning bush, one recorded talking donkey, one recorded blind man on the road to Damascus, one recorded wet fleece on dry ground, one recorded vision of food on a sheet, and one recorded revelation on the island of Patmos. Over and over again, we see God communicating in ways that reached the individual. God made communication about us hearing Him. He was creative in how He spoke so that everyone would hear Him uniquely.

Imagine if there had been more than one instance of the events I've just mentioned. Imagine there had been three burning bushes, for example. If that had been the case, we would all be looking for burning bushes, and everyone would complain that they haven't heard from God because they haven't seen a burning bush. Fortunately, this is not how it is. We do not all have to go find a burning bush, because God speaks to each one of us in a way that reaches us individually.

People still complain that they don't hear from God, but I believe that this is mostly because they're looking for Him in a box. Many expect Him to speak in a certain way, or believe that He can only be heard through the Bible. Well, let's let the Bible be our proof that God wants to speak to every individual in a way that person can hear. The Bible shows us that God will speak uniquely and individually. Stay open-minded to the "sound" of His voice.

What does all this have to do with fear? To reshape every belief we have that's been influenced by fear, we have to find out what He is saying. I keep a constant conversation in my head with God. When I face a situation where anxiety, worry, or fear arises, I listen for His voice and hear him saying things such as: "Peace, my child," "I am with you," "I have you protected," "My angels are all around," and much more. It's these moments of constant conversation that give me the declarations to live by.

- I am protected.
- I am loved.
- I have God by my side.
- I have peace and not fear.

These declarations have reshaped my life.

How Do You Join the Conversation?

I know that many of us still feel as if we can't hear the voice of God. A few paragraphs in a book may not change that right away, but I want to give you some simple starting points from my own experience.

1. You *can* hear God in the Bible.

This is a great place to start because the Bible is filled with God's promises. It's filled with Him working through messed-up lives. It's filled with redemption. It's filled with love. As long as you can read it through the lens of His character, which is Love (see 1 John 4:8), then you will hear Him speaking, as Who He really is—a God of love, longing for relationship.

2. Be aware of God in everything.

I don't believe that God is ever silent. The essence of relationship is communication, so if there is no communication, there is no relationship. Many times, when we think He is silent, it is because we are looking to hear from Him in a certain way. But the awareness of God's omnipresence creates an expectation to hear Him speak.

One day, I was driving in our community on a beautiful spring day in April. All the trees were green with lush life. I pulled up to a stoplight, and suddenly a large brown leaf landed right on my windshield on the driver's side. It stayed for a few seconds and then blew away. I could have just ignored it and moved on. But I suddenly became aware of God's presence. I looked all around for a tree with brown leaves, but nothing. They were all green. So I took a moment to check in with God and asked, "God, are you speaking to me through that leaf?" I heard Him reply to my spirit, "Yes. I'm changing the seasons early in your life." In that quick, passing moment, I had the opportunity to hear God tell me about the acceleration that was happening in my life.

On another day, I was looking for earrings to complement my outfit. They were gold heart earrings that had two dangling hearts on each. As I reached for them, one of the earrings dropped to the floor—but I still had two in my hand. There were actually three earrings! This was quite bizarre. Why did I have three heart earrings? At that moment, I became aware of the presence of God. So I asked, "God, are you speaking to me through this third earring?" I heard a reply from Him to my spirit, "You have three ears. One is your heart. Listen with your heart." Wow! I'm still processing that revelation.

God is speaking throughout the day, even in the mundane. He is all around, and paying attention to Him in your day will create opportunities for you to hear His whispers of revelation and love.

3. Realize that your great idea probably wasn't yours alone.

If we were created in the image of God, then doesn't it seem that our good thoughts and ideas would be from Him? That thoughts of love, hope, faith, patience, creativity, joy, and more stem from the Author of these? We give ourselves a lot of credit for what is actually flowing from His mind through us, but 1

Corinthians 2:16 tells us that we actually have the mind of Christ. With that said, we can begin to learn to trust the good output from our minds as the voice of God speaking to us.

These are just a few of the ways we can learn how to hear God. There are many more to be explained later in the book. Just know God will tailor His voice to your unique ear. He will not be silent, so open up your mind and heart to hear.

Conversation Becomes Freedom

When God speaks, His words can become the declarations of our lives. As Bill Johnson, the Senior Pastor of Bethel Church in Redding, California, says, "I must never have a thought in my mind about me that God does not have in His about me." This is a radical statement that carries so much truth. If I want to establish new beliefs in my life that will erase the fears to which I have become accustomed, I have to hear what God is saying about my circumstances and my destiny.

Declarations Can Release Life

Fear steals our freedom to truly live. But declarations have the power to thwart fear. When we declare the truth of what God says about us, our lives, and His love for us, life is released.

One of the first and most basic steps we can take to eliminate fear is to simply change what we say, which will change how we think, feel, and live. It's time to be intentional with our words so that we live our lives free … free of fear.

REFLECTIONS

1. It's never too late to change the way my brain functions.

Ask yourself, "What are some areas of my thinking that have been plagued with fear?"

_____

_____

_____

2. I can change any fear-based thinking by changing what I think about and declare about my life.

Ask yourself, "What are the most common negative thoughts and declarations I struggle with regarding myself and my future?"

_____

_____

_____

3. My declarations should be shaped by what God says about me.

What are some promises in the Bible that help me overcome my struggles?

_____

_____

_____

Spend some time alone with God and ask Him, "God, what do you think about me?" Write down His reply.

_____

_____

_____

CHAPTER TWO

WISDOM VS. HEALTHY FEAR:
Eradicating the Idea of "Healthy Fear"

After years of medical issues, I had developed what I called a "healthy fear" of doctors. My healthy fear made me cautious about choosing which doctor I would see. It helped me prepare mentally for what I might face. And it led me to take better care of my body, so I could *avoid* doctors.

With numerous changes in my life growing up and relational roller-coasters in my life, I also developed a healthy fear of people in general, not just doctors. My healthy fear made me wary of new people who might take advantage of me. It protected me from rejection by others. And it kept people who might want intimacy with me at bay and kept me from spending emotional energy I didn't want to spend.

Even though these "healthy fears" seemed to be protecting me, the truth was that they were making me sicker. My pet fears were only making my life more miserable. By the time I was sixteen, I was in a full-on depression. I was cutting, bulimic, and on Prozac. Many of these struggles could have been caused from the stress of my life circumstances, but the truth is that stress is simply internalized fear. My "healthy fear" was taking a toll on my life.

Is "Healthy Fear" Healthy?

Maybe you've heard the saying, "A little bit of fear is healthy." Sure, why not? Give me a little spoonful of fear for my health. What? Really?

Healthy fear is an oxymoron of confusions and lies. How can you even put the two words together? Since I lived it, I know the answer. The term "healthy fear" is no more than a justification for living with some level of fear in your life. The fear that makes you feel safe—if that makes any sense—is the fear you cling to for protection. The fear that sings you to sleep but then causes you to startle awake at the slightest sound expecting the worst. Familiar?

I've had people give me the following scenarios as proof of the necessity of healthy fear:

- "It's healthy fear that keeps you from jumping off the edge of a cliff."

- "It's healthy fear that keeps you from crashing your car into a guardrail."

- "It's healthy fear that keeps you from letting your children cross the street without holding your hand."

I'm sure that as you're reading this, you're thinking, "Absolutely! This kind of fear is good." I must disagree. No. It is not.

I want to propose a healthier option to this form of fear: wisdom. Is it possible that it should actually be *wisdom*, not fear, that keeps you from jumping off the cliff? I'll build my case— and then you can decide.

If at any point you decide to agree with fear, fear does not simply stop after that agreement is established. When you agree with fear to justify your reasoning for not jumping off a cliff, a momentum develops, and eventually you'll find yourself, perhaps twenty or thirty years later, wondering why you have a deathly fear of heights. You ask yourself, "Why don't I like elevators? Why won't I ride roller coasters anymore? Why does the idea of hiking make me anxious?" These are not healthy fears. These are destructive fears. These fears sap the vitality from your life.

Wisdom, on the other hand, is defined in Webster's Dictionary as "good sense." In the Bible, throughout the book of Proverbs, wisdom is personified repeatedly as the one who keeps us from making poor life choices. For example, as in Proverbs 8: "Does not wisdom cry out, and understanding lift up her voice? She takes her stand on the top of the high hill, beside the way, where the paths meet."

Wisdom is also described in the New Testament as being the spiritual gift of life application: "Look carefully then how you walk, not as unwise but as wise, making the best use of the time." (Ephesians 5:15)

Let's revisit the cliff scenario with wisdom in mind. It is wisdom that keeps me from jumping off the cliff. It is the innate, spiritual gift of good sense that God has given me that allows me to foresee the consequences of my choices. When I partner with wisdom, I begin to see a forward motion in my life. And as wisdom grows, I make better choices, have greater discipline, and walk in more self-control. Now that, my friends, is healthy!

Fear and Its Effects on Health

As I said before in telling my own story, fear, in even its "healthy" disguise, was still ultimately an unhealthy influence in my life. The following statistics and information offer telling evidence about the effects of fear on our health.

According to Ron Ovitt, Executive Pastor of Calvary Church in Orland Park, Illinois, in an online article on "Overcoming Fear—A Key to Health and Healing":

> In spite of what they say, 90% of the chronic patients who see today's physicians have one common symptom. Their trouble did not start with cough or chest pain or hyperacidity. In 90% of the cases, the first symptom was fear.
>
> This is the opinion of a well-known American internist as expressed in a roundtable discussion on psychosomatic medicine. This is also the consensus of a growing body of specialists. Fear of losing a job, of old age, of being exposed—sooner or later this fear manifests itself as "a clinical symptom." Diseases with a link to fear include cardiovascular diseases, hypertension, digestive-tract diseases, Crohn's disease, bowel syndromes, ulcers, headaches, skin disorders, immune dysfunctions.[1]

This is the growing consensus of more and more specialists and experts on psychosomatic medicine. Fear of losing a job, of old age, of being exposed—sooner or later these fears manifest as a clinical symptom.

Advice columnist Ann Landers used to receive an average of 10,000 letters each month from people burdened with problems.

---

[1] Ron Ovitt, "Overcoming Fear – A Key to Health and Healing," *Emotional Learning*, May 20, 2007, https://sozo1.wordpress.com/2007/05/20/overcoming-fear-a-key-to-health-and-healing

When asked if there was any one problem that dominated the letters she received, she replied, "People are afraid of losing their health, their wealth, their loved ones. People are afraid of life itself."

One documented case that demonstrates the power of the mind to manifest fear was recounted in a 2003 post on "the negative effects of fear on the mind" by minister and psychologist, Dr. Lee E. Warren:

> In *The New York Times*, July 26,1970, an article entitled "Child's Death in London Laid to Fear of Dentist" was published and also included in a book entitled Psychosomatics by Howard R. and Martha E. Lewis (© 1975 Viking Press), p. 27. A four-year-old child had a bad experience with a local anesthetic for stitches taken from her forehead. When she went to the dentist to have some baby teeth extracted, she screamed hysterically in the dentist's chair. He gave the child a sedative to quiet her for the examination. Within a few minutes after having her teeth removed, the child had a heart attack and was rushed to the hospital where she died two days later. The autopsy found very high levels of adrenaline in her blood stream due to fear that caused her to have a heart attack. Fear of the dentist resulted in the child's death. So we see excess fear can be catastrophic on a man's mind.[2]

---

[2] Howard R. and Martha Lee Lewis, "Child's Death in London Laid to Fear of Dentist," New York Times, July 26, 1970.

The Amygdala and the Fight Against Fear

I'm sure you've heard of the fight-or-flight response. Recently, the choices were expanded by the medical field to "fight, flight, or freeze." Fear is the culprit behind these unhealthy choices. I'm sure that none of you who are reading this book wants to put up your dukes, run away, or be paralyzed when facing a challenge. But how can we circumvent having to make dark and difficult choices? Before answering this question, we must understand some things about the brain.

Imagine sitting in your living room alone reading a good novel...sigh...the peace. Suddenly you hear the back door rattle violently. Two choices arise before fight, flight, or freeze even become options. You can make the wise choice to think through what might be causing the rattling—the wind, a fallen tree branch, a neighbor who needs a cup of sugar—or you can make the foolish choice of jumping to the worst conclusion—that someone is breaking into your house.

The good choice leads your brain chemistry to your sensory cortex, which takes time to interpret incoming information. The bad choice leads your brain chemistry straight to your amygdala, where your fear memories are stored.

In the good choice: when your sensory cortex is engaged, sensors then land on the hippocampus, which processes stimuli and establishes the context of your situation. (see table below)

But if you decide on the bad choice, your amygdala is triggered and it sends information to your hypothalamus, which activates the fight, flight, or freeze response—or fear (see table).

Wisdom	Fear
⬇	⬇
Sensory Cortex interprets incoming data	**Amygdala** where fear memories are stored
⬇	⬇
Hippocampus processes stimuli and establishes context	**Hypothalamus** activates fight, flight, freeze; strengthens fear circuits

According to *New York Times* science writer Carl Zimmer:

> Our exquisitely sophisticated brains may make this predator-defense circuit [for fear] vulnerable to misfiring. Instead of monitoring just the threats right in front of us, we can also imagine threats that do not exist. Feeding this imagination into the early-warning system may lead to crippling chronic anxiety. In other cases, people may not be able to keep their midbrain regions under control. As we perceive predators getting closer, our brains normally make the switch from the forebrain to the midbrain regions. People who suffer panic disorders may misjudge threats, seeing them as far more imminent than they really are.[3]

---

[3] Carl Zimmer, "The Primitive, Complicated, Essential Emotion Called Fear," *Discover Magazine*, February 16, 2010, http://discovermagazine.com/2010/jan-feb/16-primitive-complicated-essential-emotion-called-fear.

The other thing to understand about fear is that it's the *only* emotion that creates an involuntary response in the brain. If wisdom, understanding, knowledge, and revelation are all good and desirable voluntary brain responses, then anything that occurs involuntarily is not a healthy thought process. Fear signals responses that happen without thinking. Fear creates responses that are not from a place of wisdom. Fear triggers responses that are not processed with understanding. Fear forces responses that are not based on well-rounded knowledge. Fear responses do not come from any higher place of revelation or wisdom.

Fear, in fact, is the paralyzer of healthy decision-making. It is by no means healthy in and of itself.

The following are unhealthy physical symptoms that occur when the amygdala is overstimulated and fear becomes the natural response:

- Heart rate and blood pressure increase.
- Pupils dilate to take in as much light as possible.
- Veins constrict to send more blood to major muscle groups. (This causes the "chills," sometimes associated with fear due to less blood in the superficial veins of the skin to keep it warm.)
- Blood glucose levels increase.
- Muscles tense up, energized by adrenaline and glucose. (This causes goose bumps because when the tiny muscles attached to each hair on the skin tense up, the hairs are forced upright and pull the skin with them.)
- Nonessential systems (like digestion and the body's immune systems) shut down to allow more energy for emergency functions.
- Focusing on small tasks becomes difficult. (The brain is directed to focus only on the big picture in order to determine where the threat is coming from.)

As we can see from this brief discussion about the brain, how it works, our emotions, and our physical responses to fear, there is no health in a life of fear. So how can we counteract fear-influenced living? What will lead us to a path guided by wisdom?

Faith and Wisdom Are Friends

I address the subject of faith versus fear in a later chapter, but let me say this one thing before moving on from the effects of fear on the brain. When faced with fear, faith is what shifts our positive thought processes back into gear and helps to overcome the involuntary process that prompts us to fight, flight, or freeze.

The brain on faith could be described as an *expectant* brain—a brain that is expecting the best and believing that all things will work together for the good. It is more than just positive thinking—it is hope lived out.

In the previous chapter, I discussed the placebo effect, which happens when people are given a pill with no known medicinal properties but are told that it does have medicinal properties. In many cases, they experience improvements like those seen in people being treated with real medications. Beliefs do have a dynamic impact on the brain. For example, faith healing is a supernatural event that I have experienced and witnessed numerous times. The medical and science fields are beginning to take note of this as well. Faith is a huge factor in learning to live the healthier life of wisdom.

What's Your Reasoning for Living with "Healthy Fear"?

How much has fear motivated your choices in life?

- Has the fear of wrinkles caused you to spend exorbitant amounts of money on creams?

- Has the fear of hell scared you into an insincere religious commitment?
- Has the fear of being overweight limited your food choices?
- Has the fear of being hurt kept you out of intimate relationships?
- Has the fear of flying stopped you from visiting certain places?

One of the most common arguments I have heard in support of fear is that "fear pushes us to go further." Many believe it protects us from bad choices and propels us toward good ones. An example would be that fear of failure may force us to try harder. Or that fear of rejection can help us set good boundaries in our relationships. Or that fear of the police encourages us to obey the law. The problem is, if fear bypasses important processing functions in our brain, how can we believe it should be the motivating element in our decision-making? Fear may keep us from risky investments, uncertain people, and dangerous chance-taking, but what will be the effects of living with consistent doses of fear?

We can discover how consistent doses of fear affect people by examining a tool called "fear conditioning." Fear conditioning is a therapy designed to help people function in drastic and dire situations. Fear conditioning creates a behavioral paradigm in which organisms learn to predict adverse events. Fear conditioning involves forcing subjects into regularly recurring situations that are meant to invoke fear. Fear conditioning actually occurs naturally in repeated abusive situations. If a child grows up with an abusive parent, a lack of provision or bullying in school, fear conditioning becomes part of that child's diet. But fear conditioning can also be simulated to prepare the body for stressful situations such as war. Unfortunately, the results of fear conditioning are typically negative. Experimental data supports the notion that our brain develops an inability to respond correctly to the amygdala when fear conditioning occurs. In some cases, the brain forms permanent fear responses, which can develop into post-traumatic stress disorder (PTSD). Magnetic resonance imaging (MRI) and functional magnetic resonance imaging (fMRI) scans have shown that the amygdala in individuals diagnosed with such disorders as PTSD, and including bipolar or panic disorder, is larger and wired for a higher level of fear. This wiring, in many cases, came through natural or simulated fear conditioning.

When fear is a person's primary motivator, everything becomes distorted. Fear may have a seemingly temporary benefit, but it carries long-term negative side effects. Many times, the temporary, easy solution is the worst long-term solution. Good long-term solutions require an investment of energy and time. Since investment means risk, and time is precious, fear can again rear its ugly head and become the easiest choice even when you are trying to move in the opposite direction.

As mentioned above, some people believe that it's wise to use fear as a motivator. I beg to differ. I want to share one more story from the Bible that I briefly touched upon in Chapter One. It is about twelve spies who were sent to spy out a land that was promised to them by God. Upon their return from spying out the land, ten spies responded in fear and declared that no matter how rich and fruitful the land was, the giants who lived there were too powerful to overcome. The other two spies saw instead the promise of the fruits of the land in front of them. This gave them a motivation to move toward their destiny, stronger than any level of fear that could keep them away from it. It's interesting how following the promises of God and the call to live out of wisdom will result in choices that lead us into our destiny—while the decision to walk in fear will hinder us from ever reaching the destiny we were designed for.

I recently had a conversation with a woman about fear. She was sharing with me that her kids' soccer coach tells them they must respect fear because it's an authority in their lives that protects them. I proceeded to share with her the jumping-off-the-cliff analogy I mentioned earlier, and before I could even get to the point or mention wisdom, she said, "Wisdom is what should keep you from jumping off the cliff, not fear." I said, "Exactly!"

I believe it is in our innate design to base our choices in life on a foundation of wisdom. Since we are created in the image of God, the propensity for wisdom is already stamped into our DNA. But if we choose to ignore it or allow it to atrophy, other outside forces will begin trying to make a home in our minds and influencing the life choices we make. These outside forces include fear, anger, worry, and other negative motivators.

We Become What We Behold

By focusing on an idea or a concept, we allow that idea or concept to have a profound impact. We become what we behold. My favorite example of this is in 2 Corinthians 3:18: "And we all, with unveiled face, beholding the glory of the Lord, are being transformed into the same image from one degree of glory to another. For this comes from the Lord who is the Spirit."

When I read this verse, I came to understand that by simply beholding the glory of the Lord, my transformation manifests. What I choose to see and focus upon is given power in my life. It's not a striving or difficult effort-exerting process. It is simply a beholding. If I behold the wisdom of God for my life, my life will pattern itself toward a destiny of promise. But the opposite is also true. If I behold fear, I will become its victim.

The "But Rather" Method

I read a life-changing book by minister and author, Jonathan Welton, titled *Eyes of Honor*. The focus of his book is to bring hope to those struggling with sexual impurity or temptation. One section outlines what he calls the "but rather" method. He explains if you simply tell someone "Do not lust," it would be like telling someone "Do not think about an orange." What are they going to end up thinking about? An orange, of course. He then reveals that in the New Testament, Jesus Himself employed a "but rather" method in which He offered a second option to engage the mind. For example, Welton would say, "Do not think about an orange, but rather think about an elephant"; or "Do not lust, but rather pray for the women caught up in the traps of the sex industry."

Here are some Bible scriptures that Welton offers as examples of this method:

- Don't use freedom to wallow in sin, but rather serve one another in love. (Galatians 5: 13)

- Don't be obscene, foolish, or coarse; but rather give thanks. (Ephesians 5: 4)

- Don't become enslaved to philosophy, but rather follow Christ. (Colossians 2: 8)

- Don't get caught up in controversies, but rather focus on God's work. (1 Timothy 1: 4)

- Don't gossip, but rather train yourself to be godly. (1Timothy 4: 7)

- Don't be sinful, but rather be lovers of God. (2 Timothy 3: 4)

- Don't be disabled, but rather healed. (Hebrews 12: 13)

- Don't live for earthly desires, but rather for the will of God. (1 Peter 4: 2)

- Don't be involved in sexual immorality, but rather clothe yourself with Christ. (Romans 13: 14)[4]

I choose to live in line with the above "but rather" examples by saying the following:

- Do not fear, but rather trust in God.

- Do not fear, but rather speak peace over your life.

- Do not fear, but rather hope in all the promises God has.

- Do not fear, but rather choose wisdom.

Willing myself to not be afraid will only cause me to think about fear. But beholding the next rung on the ladder that I can reach for will allow me to forget about the obstacles below. I believe this "but rather" method is inspired and unlocks gifts of wisdom.

Fear in Heaven?

Here is a very simple question to sum up this topic on the existence of healthy fear: Is there *fear* in heaven? If your answer is no, then you're agreeing that fear should have no place in your life. If your answer is yes, then I would not want to go to your heaven.

Why do I state this so strongly? Jesus shows us a prayer in Matthew 6 that is meant to infuse the way we live every day of our lives. My favorite verse in the prayer is verse 10—"Your kingdom come, Your will be done, on earth as it is in heaven"

---

[4] Jonathan Welton, *Eyes of Honor: Training for Purity and Righteousness* (Shippensburg, PA: Destiny Image Publishers, 2012), Kindle Edition.

(Matthew 6:10)—because here Jesus is saying that we are to pray that earth looks and operates like heaven. We are to believe that to experience His kingdom and His will, we must pray that things happen on earth as they happen in Heaven. Jesus doesn't have a reputation for being ironic. I don't think He gave us this verse to tell us that we can pray this way if we like, but it's not going to do us any good. Jesus gave us this because Heaven on earth is not only attainable and possible, it's the goal. If there is no fear in Heaven, then the goal is for there to be no fear on earth.

Is there wisdom in Heaven? My answer is a resounding yes! In fact, each and every aspect of Heaven was created with wisdom, for in Heaven lie the answers and strategies for earth and for our individual lives. His Kingdom come will look like solutions to cancer, the ending of poverty, answers to crises, and every possible wisdom-infused revelation. His will being done will look like us living out these heavenly strategies and revelations. Wisdom is the propeller that we must make sure is attached to the plane we're on. In partnering with wisdom, not only will we experience the decrease of fear in our life, we will see the increase of faith for all possibilities.

REFLECTIONS

In this chapter, we have learned that:

1. Fear is never healthy in our lives.

Ask yourself, "What are some areas in my life where I've used fear as way to protect myself?"

_____

_____

_____

2. Fear paralyzes healthy decision-making. Wisdom is the place we make our life decisions from.

Meditate on certain areas of your life (relationships, family, work, etc.). Ask yourself how wisdom might better guide your life.

_____

_____

_____

3. Focus not on fear, but rather on the destiny in store for us.

Write your own "but rather" statements regarding areas where you need freedom from fear.

_____

_____

_____

4. There is no fear in heaven, so there should be no fear on earth.

Take some time alone with God and ask Him to show you the riches of Heaven. Write down some of the revelations He gives you.

_____

_____

_____

CHAPTER THREE

Discovering the Truth About "The Fear of God"

I was seventeen years old and sitting in a church service voluntarily for the first time in two years. I had spent those previous two years drinking, using drugs, getting involved with the wrong guys, and skipping school. I had gone from being a straight-A student, cheerleader, and class president to a troubled girl who had been kicked out of high school and was on the wrong track. During those years, I ignored God, searching instead for something that made me feel alive.

So there I was, choosing to come back to church. The sermon was strong and mighty, and I felt moved. I felt moved by *something*, anyway. The preacher told me that if we didn't repent, God would destroy everything in our lives until we did. He used many Old Testament examples of how God had killed and abused those who didn't "get right" with Him. The "something" I felt in the service that day was not love, hope, or grace. It was fear. It was that old familiar security blanket that brought me running back.

The fear of God has been a popular motivator used by churches and religions for centuries. Many of us find ourselves in a relationship with God today because of that motivator. The problem is that if you were saved by fear, you must be kept by fear. If it's fear that motivates you, then it's fear that will have to keep motivating you. And because you've built your spiritual foundation on fear, you may find yourself mired in rebellion, guilt, shame, and re-commitment for the rest of your life.

There is no place for fear in your relationship with God. If there's even a trace of fear, you will never feel free.

The fear of God is perhaps the strongest argument supporting the beneficial effects of having some form of fear in your life. I believe that the fear of God is the most misunderstood concept in religion. We hold to this fear as if it were a sacred cow. After interviewing many, I've discovered that the fear of God creates anxiety in most people. There's something in our brains, and I believe also in our spirits, that is constantly asking, "Am I really supposed to fear God?" It's incredibly confusing to try to reconcile fearing God with the New Testament scriptures: "Perfect loves casts out fear." (1 John 4:18) and "God has not given you a spirit of fear." (2 Timothy 1:7)

Here are some common theological explanations used for the fear of God:

- Fear is reverence or awe.
- We must fear God's discipline. God disciplines those He loves.
- We should fear God because of our sin. God hates the sin but loves the sinner.

I find no peace in any of these explanations. One of my core values is that any interpretation of the Bible that does not create peace in my spirit reveals there is a greater understanding that I do not yet have but am called to pursue and discover. The fear of God has been something very unsettling to my spirit, especially because I've spent most of my life plagued by other fears.

I used to be someone who woke up in the middle of the night certain that a tsunami was heading right toward me. I was someone who would check the knob on my gas stove thirteen times just to make sure it was off before I went to sleep. I obsessively checked under my bed, behind my shower curtain, in my closet, and through my peephole. I woke up with panic attacks. I imagined myself dying. I had visions of my children being fatally wounded. It was a miserable existence that I worked tirelessly to overcome through inner healing, deliverance, counseling, etc. So the idea of keeping some measure of fear in my life concerning the one person I should trust – God – did not make sense to me.

The Revelation That Changed It All

Our church, The Church at Parkview, has an annual women's retreat that is always inspirational. But to call the 2009 retreat inspirational would be putting it mildly—it was life-changing. God showed up in ways that I could not comprehend. His presence was powerful and strong.

On the Saturday night of the retreat, the night before I was to teach, I was in my room preparing my message when I realized I had left my Bible in the meeting room. The meeting room was only about a hundred yards from my room, but getting there meant traversing snake-infested woods in the dark of night. And I had a deathly fear of snakes. But I felt such a strong impression to go get my Bible that I went anyway, running and trembling the whole way. Bible in hand, I came back to my room, let the adrenaline subside, and sat pondering the whole scenario. A few minutes later, I began feeling as if God had something He wanted to show me about fear in that very moment. I felt compelled to search the topic "The Fear of God" on the Internet.

Because the retreat center was deep in the woods of Northern California, Internet reception was intermittent—but, miraculously I had full Internet reception at that moment. I typed "The Fear of God" into the Google search box. The very first listing contained original Hebrew text from the Old Testament along with an analysis of the interpretation. What I was about to read would change my life forever.

In the past, I had researched "The Fear of God" many times with very little change in my search results except for the aforementioned common theological explanations. I had taken two years of Greek, but never Hebrew, so I had always depended upon the insights, education, and experience of others to deepen my understanding of the scriptures of the Old Testament.

This search result from Hebrew scholars was a gold mine.

I came across explanations and articles that began explaining the Hebrew word *yara*, translated as fear. *Yara* is defined as "flowings." Many times, the word is used to describe rain, as in "the flowing of rain." It's is also often used for emotions, as in "a flowing of emotions." In this article, there was reference to it meaning a flowing from the gut, since Hebrews believe that the gut is the seat of their emotions:

- When we're *afraid*, our gut flows or stirs. When I'm fearful, I sometimes feel as if I want to throw up.

- When we're in *awe*, our gut stirs. When I look at the X2 roller coaster at Magic Mountain, I get butterflies.

- When we're in *love*, our gut also flows. I have felt my insides in knots over the depth of love I feel for someone.

Whether flowings are from the gut, from my emotions, or simply rain, the renewed understanding of *yara* is something other than fear.

But which of these is the correct interpretation of *yara*/flowings: fear, awe, or love? Let's examine one very popular verse to find the answer: "The Fear of the Lord is the beginning of wisdom; and knowledge of the Holy One is understanding." (Proverbs 9:10, New International Version) In this scripture, fear is *yirah*, from the root word *yara*. The first concept to grasp in this scripture is that fear is a form of the word "flowings." I also discovered that *yirah* is understood to represent one's sensitivity to the presence of another. So not only is this scripture referencing flowings; it is also referencing flowings that are prompted by the presence of others. This communicates the essence of relationship, intimacy, and connection.

In addition, and probably most importantly, when you put two Hebrew nouns together in certain phrasings, the second noun possesses the first noun grammatically. This is referred to as being written in a "construct state." Proverbs 9:10 is written in a construct state. Here are some other examples to more clearly explain:

- The Word of the Lord = The Lord's Word
- The Name of the Lord = The Lord's Name
- The Blessing of the Lord = The Lord's Blessing

You see where I'm going, don't you?

The Fear of the Lord = The Lord's Fear

The Fear of the Lord is not our fear. It's His. We're talking about what flows from Him. Look at this example from Psalm 19:7-9 to confirm this truth (emphases added):

"The law of the Lord is perfect, reviving the soul; the testimony of the Lord is sure, making wise the simple; the precepts of the Lord are right, rejoicing the heart; the commandment of the Lord is pure, enlightening the eyes; *the fear of the Lord is clean*, enduring forever; the rules of the Lord are true, and righteous altogether."

When we read this, it's common sense that the law of the Lord, the testimony of the Lord, the precepts of the Lord, the commandment of the Lord, and the rules of the Lord are all possessed by the Lord. They are His. But when we get to the *fear* of the Lord, our misinterpretation says it's *our* fear. In the train of thought communicated in this scripture, that understanding is inconsistent with the structure of the rest. The fear of the Lord must be the Lord's. And if it is His, it couldn't be fear.

Let's go back to the first part of Proverbs 9:10 and rephrase it into a more accurate interpretation: "What flows from God is the beginning of wisdom...."

The beautiful part of this verse is that within it lies a natural confirmation of its true meaning. Look at the second part of the proverb: "The Fear of the Lord is the beginning of wisdom; *and knowledge of the Holy One is understanding.*" Hebrew poetry often uses parallelism as a literary device. Parallelism is where the words of two or more lines of text are directly related in some way. This feature can be found in many poetic passages and sometimes even in narratives, although it's more common in the Psalms and Proverbs. It's a tool meant to emphasize the impact of the passage. The phrase "knowledge of the Holy One is understanding" or, literally, "*[knowing]* the Holy One is understanding" is parallel to the idea that getting in touch with what flows from God is the beginning of wisdom. The verse itself contains a direct affirmation to a renewed understanding of the fear of the Lord. And the word "knowing" in the second half of this verse is the Hebrew verb *yada*, which is a euphemism for sexual intimacy. Essentially, that second portion of the verse means "know Him intimately":

The flowings of God are the beginning of wisdom, and knowing him intimately is understanding.

I believe that Proverbs 9:10 is simply an invitation to know intimately what flows from the heart and mind of God. In accepting that invitation, we will find ourselves growing in wisdom and understanding. Fear is removed from the picture. There is no fear of God.

I encourage you to challenge your current understanding of the Fear of the Lord. My guess is after reading this, you may feel sure that it's blasphemy to think about doing so. In fact, as you remember what you may have previously believed, you might even feel afraid to accept this challenge. Continue to do your own study and research. I recommend Jeff A. Benner and his Ancient Hebrew Research Center (www.ancient-hebrew.org) to find great info and links to many great resources.

I'm not going to stop here in addressing fear in the Bible. I've researched every mention of fear in the Bible. It became my life mission for a period of time, because I knew that if there was any element of fear in my relationship with God, I would never feel free from fear in my life. I knew I had to discover what the Biblical texts were truly revealing about God, about me, and about fear.

Fear in the Old Testament

In the Old Testament, the Hebrew root word *yara* and its many forms (*yare, yirah, yare hayah, yirat*) are mentioned more than one hundred times. We can take our renewed understanding of "flowings" and apply it to numerous scriptures in the Old

Testament, for example: "He will bless those who fear the LORD, both small and great." (Psalms 115:13)

Again, the word *yara* means a flowing from the individual: "He will bless those who are *moved emotionally by the Lord*" is a better interpretation.

Here are some other scriptures that relate to the study of *yara* in the Bible:

"You shall not curse the deaf or put a stumbling block before the blind, but you shall fear [*yare* (verb)] your God: I am the Lord." (Leviticus 19:14, New King James Version)	New understanding: "You shall not curse the deaf or put a stumbling block before the blind, but you shall be moved by your God: I am the Lord."
"Oh that they had such a heart in them that they would fear [*yira* (verb), in relation to sensitivity to another always] Me and always keep My commandments, that it might be well with them and with their children forever!" (Deuteronomy 5:29, New King James Version)	New understanding: "Oh that they had such a heart in them to be moved by Me and to keep all My commandments, that it might go well with them and with their descendants forever!"
"The God of Israel has spoken; the Rock of Israel has said to me: 'When one rules justly over men, ruling in the fear [yirah (possessive noun-construct form)] of God.'" (2 Samuel 23:3, English Standard Version)	New understanding: "The God of Israel has spoken; the Rock of Israel has said to me: 'When one rules justly over men, ruling in what flows from God.'"

"And he said to man, 'Behold, the fear [yirat (possessive noun-construct form)] of the Lord, that is wisdom, and to turn away from evil is understanding.'" (Job 28:28, English Standard Version)	New understanding: "And he said to man, 'Behold, what flows from the Lord, that is wisdom, and to turn away from evil is understanding.'"
"Come, O children, listen to me; I will teach you the fear [yirat (possessive noun-construct form)] of the Lord." (Psalms 34:11, English Standard Version)	New understanding: "Come, O children, listen to me; I will teach you what flows from the Lord."
"In the fear [yirah (possessive noun-construct form)] of the Lord one has strong con-fidence, and His children will have a refuge." (Proverbs 14:26 English Standard Version)	New understanding: "In what flows from the Lord one has strong confidence, and His children will have a re-fuge."
"And the Spirit of the Lord shall rest upon him, the Spirit of wisdom and understanding, the Spirit of counsel and might, the Spirit of knowledge and the fear [yirat (possessive noun-construct form)] of the Lord." (Isaiah 11:2, English Standard Version)	New understanding: "And the Spirit of the Lord shall rest upon him, the Spirit of wisdom and understanding, the Spirit of counsel and might, the Spirit of knowledge and what flows from the Lord."

These are only a handful of the scriptures that are worth rethinking. I've spoken with Hebrew scholars who agree that *yara* means "flowings." Many of our concordances do not reflect the true meaning of Hebrew and Greek words. Also, we often don't have the English words to convey the deep meaning of the Hebrew or Greek words in the Bible, and so we've settled for inaccurate and confusing interpretations that have been passed down from generation to generation.

Other Forms of Fear in the Bible

You'll see other uses of the word "fear" in the Bible that have nothing to do with *yara*. For example, one word, *pahad* or *phad*, can mean fearing, trembling, or standing in awe. According to some Hebrew scholars, it can even be understood as God's goodness being so overwhelming that we shake in His presence.

We see *pahad* and its variations used in the Old Testament worth examining (emphases added):

"And the fear of the Lord fell upon all the kingdoms of the lands that were around Judah, and they made no war against Jehoshaphat." (2 Chronicles 17:10, English Standard Version)	This phrasing of "fear of the Lord" is in the possessive noun-construct state, so it is again "the Lord's fear." And if it is the Lord's, it's most likely not fear but a trembling or shaking of the Lord's. You'll see this example repeated throughout 2 Chronicles.
"For the thing that I fear comes upon me, and what I dread befalls me." (Job 3:25, English Standard Version)	"Fear" in this verse is accurately translated. Job had been living in a state of fear that his life would deteriorate. This use of *pahad* is the verb form, *pahadti*, which means "the fear that I fear." You will see this Hebrew root word used throughout Job.

Below are three other scriptures that have been translated as the English word "fear" although the Hebrew words are different (emphases added):

"I sought the Lord, and He answered me and delivered me from all my *fears*." (Psalm 34:4, English Standard Version)	This root word is *meguwrah* and means "terror." The new understanding would be: "I sought the Lord, and He answered me and delivered me from all my terrors."
"The *fear of man* lays a snare, but whoever trusts in the Lord is safe." (Proverbs 29:25, English Standard Version)	The Hebrew word *charadah* means "anxiety." In this verse, it is in the possessive noun-construct state, so it is "man's anxiety." The true under-standing would be: "Man's anxiety lays a snare, but whoever trusts in the Lord is safe."
"But the Lord of hosts, Him you shall honor as holy. Let Him be your *fear*, and let Him be your *dread*." (Isaiah 8:13, English Standard Version)	In this verse, "fear" is *mowra*, which means an object of reverence. The true under-standing of this verse would be: "But the Lord of hosts, Him you shall honor as holy. Let Him be your object of reverence, and let Him be treated with awe." In the second phrase, "dread" is a translation of the verb *arats*, which means "to regard or treat with awe."

After studying the scriptures, I'm convinced that God never intended for us to live in fear. However, many scriptures in the Old and New Testament have been incorrectly translated in a manner that implies otherwise.

What Can We Conclude?

Another one of my passions is to understand and articulate the heart of God. My goal is not to try to convince you that my interpretations should be your new guide, but my research and my conversations with scholars and theologians have led me to conclude that fear was and is not in the heart of God.

If we seek after the depths of what moves God—which is His unconditional, undying love for us—we will begin to scratch the surface of true wisdom. If we can know the heart of the Holy One intimately, we will take the first steps on the path to true understanding. Let's challenge ourselves to rethink Proverbs 9:10 as well as every other verse about the "fear of God."

The conclusion of this chapter is that God is not the author of fear. He is not a perpetuator of fear. We are not supposed to fear Him. This is news for many, but it's news worth focusing on until our minds are renewed to the truth.

REFLECTIONS

In this chapter, we have learned that:

1. The words "the fear of the Lord" actually mean "flowings from God," and getting in touch with that is the beginning of wisdom.

Spend some time alone with God and ask Him to show you the things that move Him, that flow from His heart and mind. Write down what He reveals, and watch your life grow in wisdom.

_____

_____

_____

2. God is love, and it is never His heart to invoke fear in others.

Ask yourself, "What are some misconceptions I've believed about God that relate to Him being someone I should fear?"

_____

_____

_____

CHAPTER FOUR

The Fear of God, Part Two

The Old Testament was full of scriptures about "fear" that may have been mistranslated or misunderstood. Having cleared up these misinterpretations, I find myself living in more freedom. My heart feels safe in God's presence. My life feels safe in His arms. My mind has aligned itself with truth. The truth is that my God is love.

I can't leave this subject, though, without addressing some the stories and scenarios in the New Testament that have the potential to induce fear as well. So let's take some time to make sure that fear in our relationship with God is completely conquered by addressing these New Testament scriptures as well.

Ananias and Sapphira

The story of betrayal and deceit in the pages of Acts, Chapter Five, has the potential to pull us into fear. In this chapter, Ananias and Sapphira held back a portion of the money they had promised to God. After verbal exchanges with the Apostles, both of them fell down dead. Seeing that two people were struck down for lying can certainly make us begin to fear what God may do regarding the choices in our lives. When we see two people struck down for lying about giving, we might all begin to fear God, because He could strike us down when He is displeased with us.

Before diving into the mystery of these two fascinating characters, let's consider a few things. The belief that God will strike you down requires the belief that God is in control. Whatever good or bad happens, God is in control of it...right? I can hear the arguing voices going off even as I type:

> "Well, that's right! God *is* in control!"

> "Don't even *begin* to tell me God's not in control!"

> "I'm going to shut this book right now and never open it again if you tell me God's *not* in control!"

Guess what? God is *not* in control.

God is in charge.

There's a huge difference. Breathe and stay with me. "Control" isn't a flattering word. Do you like to be controlled? I think not. Control is a tool that comes into play when fear is involved. We only control when we fear things that are out of our control. Just the sheer fact that God has given us a will to make our own choices is proof that He is not out to control us. In fact, He wants us to learn *self-control*. Self-control is a fruit of the Spirit; trying to control others is not.

This issue of "God being in control" is the reason for a great deal of questioning in the world:

> "Why does God send suffering?"

> "Why does God allow bad things to happen to good people?"

> "Why did God orchestrate this chaos in my life?"

Poor God. This issue of Him being in control is causing Him to be blamed for things that were never His intent—or His doing.

With our will, we make choices. With our will, we allow bad things to happen. With our will, others make bad choices that affect good people in negative ways. Many times people will ask the question, "Why did God allow this?" But maybe God is asking, "Why did you allow this?" Maybe we are asking an unreasonable question, since He has given us the authority, responsibility, and dominion over the earth.

Now, we do have a God who is *in charge*. He has charge over all things. He can use anything in His charge to bring about good from the nastiest of circumstances and the worst of choices. We all love Romans 8:28 for that reason: "And we know that God causes everything to work together for the good of those who love God and are called according to His purpose for them." We tend to read this scripture and think that God caused the bad and used it for good. But that's not what it says. It says that God causes everything that happens to you (no matter from what source, whether good or bad) to work together for good. He takes the bad that comes our way and turns it into something beautiful.

God's being in charge equates to His authority for bringing about a result that's in line with His character. And his ultimate character trait is *love:* "Anyone who does not love does not know God, because God is love." (1 John 4:8) Love is the only trait in the whole Bible that is personified through God. He embodies many other qualities—peace, patience, kindness, and more—but He *is* love. Any outcomes from His charge over the universe will be motivated by that love.

So if God wasn't in control of the scenario of Ananias and Sapphira in Acts 5, who was? Let's consider Peter, and the curse he spoke over Ananias:

"But Peter said, 'Ananias, why has *Satan filled your heart* to lie to the Holy Spirit and to keep back for yourself part of the proceeds of the land? While it remained unsold, did it not remain your own? And after it was sold, was it not at your disposal? Why is it that you have contrived this deed in your heart? You have not lied to man but to God.' When Ananias heard these words, he fell down and breathed his last. And great fear came upon all who heard of it." (Acts 5:3-5) (emphases added)

The power of life and death lies in what we say. Proverbs backs that up succinctly. Remember, "Death and life are in the power of the tongue, and those who love it will eat its fruits." (Proverbs 18:21) As we discussed in Chapter One, God gave us control over the fruit of our own lives through the power of our tongue. I personally feel that Peter's response, with the use of his powerful tongue, created a result in Ananias' life that wasn't God's will or heart. Peter went straight for the arrow of accusation with his powerful words. He accused Ananias of being filled with Satan himself, and he left no room or time for repentance on the part of Ananias or Sapphira. It was too late.

Confirmation for this revelation that God never intended for Ananias and Sapphira to die is found directly within the scriptures. The result of their deaths was fear: "And great fear came upon the whole church and upon all who heard of these things." (Acts 5:11) This reference to fear in verse 11 is not the Hebrew word *yara*, which means "flowings." It is the Greek word *phobos*, which means "terror." So terror came upon the church. How is that productive? And how does fear being perpetuated in the church promote the heart of God? How can a God Whose perfect love casts out fear operate effectively in a fear-filled atmosphere? I propose that it was never meant to.

God's Documentary

I am of the personal belief that the Bible is not God's literal commentary on how we should live life. Now, certainly, there are standards to live by throughout the Bible, as a commentary would imply. We have been given the Spirit of God to help reveal those standards. But throughout the Word of God are plenty of bad examples on how to live—failures, screw-ups, sin, etc.—that are not good standards for living. Just because something is in the Bible does not mean that we have to model our behavior after every individual life and action recorded. For example, Esther in the Old Testament literally slept her way to the top. Esther had to save her people by joining a royal tryout to be the queen. Is her story a standard of how we should live life? No! But it is a beautiful display of how God redeemed the culture and the circumstances to save a nation.

I believe that the Bible is more God's documentary on how He works and operates in the midst of all things, including our screw-ups. We get to know Him and His desire for a powerful destiny for each one of us throughout the Old and New Testaments. We see Him as a God Who did not control people but made them powerful enough to make their own choices. We also see a God Who takes their bad choices and redeems them for His glory.

God worked despite Peter's mistake in Acts 5:3-5. And in verse 12, he moved right along and allowed the power that the Apostles carried to be used for good—as it says, they "did many signs and wonders." (Acts 5:12) Summed up, these stories in the Bible could be, "We mess up, and His love cleans it up." I have never been comfortable accepting the death of Ananias and Sapphira as God's heart and desire, because it perpetuates fear.
Even if my interpretation of the story of Ananias and Sapphira is incorrect, I still don't believe it was God's desire for them to die. I've heard it said that the guilt that they carried may have brought their own deaths upon themselves. Or maybe they felt

so much fear that a dose of adrenaline rushed to their hearts and killed them, like the child who died of fear in the incident I recounted in Chapter Two. No one really can know for sure. What I do know is that my God of love did not kill Ananias and Sapphira to promote fear in the church.

Remember my core value about the Fear of God that I stated in Chapter Three:

> Any interpretation of the Word of God that does not create peace in my spirit reveals there is a greater understanding that I do not yet have. I am called to pursue and discover that greater understanding.

Peace is "a fruit of the Spirit." (see Galatians 5:22) Peace is also a revelation of the Kingdom of God (see Romans 14:17). When I discover the heart of God on a matter, peace results. I encourage you to reconsider the story of Ananias and Sapphira if your current understanding gives you the same lack of peace that I lived with.

Fear Throughout the New Testament

Let's look at another example in the New Testament where fear is mentioned.

> "Then the churches throughout all Judea, Galilee, and Samaria had peace and were edified. And walking in the *fear* of the Lord and in the comfort of the Holy Spirit, they were multiplied." (Acts 9:31) (emphasis added)

This common use of "fear" in the New Testament is not the Greek word *phobos*, which means "terror." It is *phoboo*, which comes from the same root but literally means "reverence for one's husband." In every place in the New Testament where "fear" is mentioned in an oddly positive way, the term *phoboo*, "reverence for one's husband," is used. And in every place where it is negative, *phobos* is used, as it should be. A small perspective change creates a huge mindset shift.

Does God Speak with Fear?

If you're a person who senses or feels atmospheres around you, then I'm guessing you've experienced some of the same confusions I have. As a woman, I naturally move by my intuition and premonition. I'm also someone who experiences God through my feelings and senses.

As someone who struggled with fear for much of my life this created an intense battle for me. When I would wake up in the middle of the night with the overwhelming fear that a tsunami was coming, I would wonder if God was warning me. If I had an image of my child not living through the night, I would wonder if God was speaking. For the longest time, I thought He was. For some reason, the knowledge that "God gave us not a spirit of fear" (see 2 Timothy 1:7) didn't settle in as a truth for my life . . . until I had a two-fold revelation from God that:

1) If perfect love casts out fear and God is love, then fear is *never* from God.

2) God would never speak in a voice contrary to His character.

So God will not speak in fear . . . or violence, or perversion, or hatred—or insecurity, for that matter. Fear is not of Him or from Him or in Him, so why would I ever think that when I feel fear, it would be His way of speaking?

Instead, God speaks to me in peace. I can actually hear Him say, "Peace, My child," whenever I feel fear. I turn to His voice and only hear peace. It's that peace that removes fear in even the scariest of situations.

This revelation leads to a very important question. Does God ever warn us of potentially frightening events and occurrences? I believe He absolutely does. But with the warning, He also reveals solutions. And those solutions will create peace and confidence in Him, not fear. Let's look at some Biblical examples, and then I'll share my most closely-related personal example.

Agabus

In Acts 11:27-30, a prophet named Agabus was warned of a great famine coming to the Roman world. But he didn't follow up this warning by inducing fear. Instead, he knew that those listening to him had the solution—they could send relief to counteract the famine. And so they did. After he offered his prophecy, no one lived in fear, there was no chaos, and there was no destruction. His listeners were equipped with the solution, and the famine was never mentioned again. If God is with us, then you had better believe that every solution to every problem is with us as well. Warnings will not come your way without accompanying hope-filled answers.

Apostle Paul

In a good portion of the New Testament, the Apostle Paul addresses potentially destructive situations: in the church, out of the church, in our character, in our relationships, etc. But in every destructive possibility lies the answer and revelation for victory in those situations. In his admonitions, Paul delivers solutions as well. To mention just a few examples:

- Living apart from the law is remedied by living by grace.

- Dealing with sexual sin in the church is handled through exposure and confrontation.

- Unforgiveness is dealt with using strategies for forgiving.

- Disunity is diminished with a call to one faith for all.

- Pride is addressed with tools to develop character.

- Persecution is overcome with the strength God gives in our weakness.

- Physical ailments are countered with the power to heal.

- Struggles in marriage and in singleness are directly discussed with options for both.

- Loss of hope is removed when people are awakened to life in Jesus.

Paul gets real about life without instilling fear. Instead, he offers the wisdom found inside every believer.

My Fears vs. My God

As I've mentioned a few times, I've had a lifelong history of irrational fear of natural disasters. When I moved to California in 2004, the irrational fear took on a much more specific focus on earthquakes and tsunamis. I remember one night in particular being awoken at around 2 a.m. with the fear that a tsunami was coming. I jumped on the Internet and began researching seismic activity and the movement of the tides. Nothing could allay my fear. My searching only increased it. I was convinced that not finding anything only meant that it had not yet been recorded and that we would all be surprised, suddenly overtaken by a large wave at any moment. I could not go back to sleep that night.

I went on having experiences like that off and on in California until I learned something. Jesus said we would do greater works than He did, and he stopped a violent storm with one phrase. So I must believe that with the resurrected Jesus within me, I have authority over the earth. He did give Adam and Eve dominion over the earth in the Garden of Eden, and if Jesus's death and resurrection bought back that dominion, then I, too, must have some power to exercise.

It was at this point in my life that I felt a personal draw to begin speaking truth over the fault lines in California. I began a daily process of declaring that all the pressure in the earth was being released slowly and incrementally and that there would be no life-destroying earthquakes or tsunamis in California. To this day, I enjoy these declarations. It is my God-given solution.

This may sound silly or ineffective, but God is always gracious enough to give confirmation in the areas where you feel a little crazy in your obedience (think Noah and the Ark). One morning in 2013, I woke up at about 7 a.m. and felt as if the nightly declarations I normally say regarding earthquakes and tsunamis needed to be said right then. So, half awake, I began to mumble over the fault lines and pressure and to pray for life, and then I fell back asleep. I didn't feel much power in that prayer but was obedient anyway. And I learned when I woke up for the day at 8 a.m. that obedience was all that had been needed.

My husband asked me, "Did you feel the earthquake?"

"What earthquake?"

"There was a 5.3 earthquake about thirty miles away from us."

I was blown away. I slowly remembered that thirty minutes before the earthquake had struck our area, I had felt compelled to declare while half-awake. But here's the thing: I had never prayed against life-destroying earthquakes and tsunamis in the morning—ever. I had only declared those things at night. But that morning God completely confirmed to me that I am hearing Him and that my obedience is not silly. Anything stronger than a 5.3 could have been quite dangerous and destructive. And I take credit (with God, of course) for the nonviolent earth-shaking that took no lives. When I trust in God's solution and listen to His voice, I live victoriously and without fear.

God has solutions for you in every area where you feel fear. Eric Johnson, Senior Leader of Bethel Church in Redding , CA, says, "The reason you are attracted to certain problems is because the solution is inside of you waiting to get out." We were not created to live lives of fear and worry and stress, and yet our society puts those ingredients in our diet on a daily basis. In John 10:10, Jesus says that He came so we could live an abundant life. Is fear keeping you from abundance? Is fear keeping you from solutions? Is fear keeping you from peace?

The Fear of God and Its Effect on Your Destiny

The parable of the three servants (Matthew 25:14-28, New Living Translation), the story of a master who entrusted financial gifts to his servants, tells a story about fear and how it can hinder us from moving forward in life:

> "Again, the Kingdom of Heaven can be illustrated by the story of a man going on a long trip. He called together his servants and entrusted his money to them while he was gone. He gave five bags of silver to one, two bags of silver to another, and one bag of silver to the last—dividing it in proportion to their abilities. He then left on his trip. The servant who received the five bags of silver began to invest the money and earned five more. The servant with two bags of silver also went to work and earned two

more. But the servant who received the one bag of silver dug a hole in the ground and hid the master's money.

After a long time their master returned from his trip and called them to give an account of how they had used his money. The servant to whom he had entrusted the five bags of silver came forward with five more and said, "Master, you gave me five bags of silver to invest, and I have earned five more." The master was full of praise. "Well done, my good and faithful servant. You have been faithful in handling this small amount, so now I will give you many more responsibilities. Let's celebrate to-gether!"

The servant who had received the two bags of silver came forward and said, "Master, you gave me two bags of silver to invest, and I have earned two more." The master said, "Well done, my good and faithful servant. You have been faithful in handling this small amount, so now I will give you many more responsibilities. Let's celebrate together!"

Then the servant with the one bag of silver came and said, "Master, I knew you were a harsh man, harvesting crops you didn't plant and gathering crops you didn't cultivate. I was afraid I would lose your money, so I hid it in the earth. Look, here is your money back." But the master replied, "You wicked and lazy servant! If you knew I harvested crops I didn't plant and gathered crops I didn't cultivate, why didn't you deposit my money in the bank? At least I could have gotten some interest on it." Then he ordered, "Take the money from this servant, and give it to the one with the ten bags of silver.'"

You'll notice that the servant who chose against investing what he had been given did not do so because he was *afraid* of his master. It was fear that actually hurt him. It was fear that kept him from taking risk. It wasn't even the risk that scared him as much as what his master would do to him if he failed. It was fear that affected his view of his master, believing he was a harsh man, not able to see his master's generosity past his own personal fear. This is an excellent example in the New Testament of fear in its true light and with its true effect.

I once heard someone say that you should fear God the way you fear your wife: "I fear what my wife would do to me if I cheated on her." But if fear is the only thing keeping you faithful, you have much bigger problems in your marriage. If we go back to fear being understood as "flowings"—which can also be caused by love—the result falls much more in line with God's heart for us. I hope my husband doesn't cheat on me, not because he's afraid of me but because he loves me. I long for love to be the motivator in our relationship. May his love for me be what guides him to protect my heart. May he be so moved by love that it compels and overwhelms him to live out that love in his behavior.

I have to believe that God wants that in our relationship with Him as well. Why would God want us to behave out of fear of Him rather than love for Him? I believe that He longs for love to be the motivator in our relationships—that we're so *moved* by love for Him that it compels and overwhelms us to live out our love in our behavior.

And do you know what sparks our love for Him?

Truly understanding His love for us.

REFLECTIONS

In this chapter, we learned that:

1. It has never been the heart of God to invoke fear in us.

Write down areas, specifically around personal struggles, that you've tried to hide from God due to fear of what He might do to you. Ask Him to show you what it looks like when His love is applied to those areas instead. Spend some time journaling this conversation.

_____

_____

_____

_____

2. God has solutions for every problem and fear.

Write down promises of God and declare them over problematic areas of fear in your life.

_____

_____

_____

_____

CHAPTER FIVE

Faith and Fear:
Replacing Fear with Faith

The thing always happens that you really believe in; and the belief in a thing makes it happen.
Frank Lloyd Wright

How often have you been asked—or asked yourself this question:

> "If you had all money in the world and no fear, what would you do with your life?"

I've heard this asked in various ways, and while I love what it stirs up with regard to dreaming and destiny and hope, I think I'm most intrigued by the question itself. It implies that fear is a major player that can block us from fulfilling our intended destinies and passions.

When I reflect on some of my own dreams, I immediately hear the fear-generated arguments rearing their ugly heads: "You aren't qualified." "You're a woman." "You don't have enough education." "You won't be provided for, and your kids will go hungry." "You're crazy." "You're too old." "You're too young." "You're not attractive enough." "Your past is too sordid."

You thought I was reading your mind for a minute there, didn't you? But all those thoughts have been my own—familiar whispers of fear that I've heard too many times. Those whispers of fear are aimed at keeping you from freedom and accomplishment.

- Fear will keep you from the book you're supposed to write.

- Fear will keep you from the business you're supposed to start.

- Fear will keep you from the relationship you're meant to have.

- Fear will keep you from the community you're meant to be engaged in.

- Fear will keep you from your bucket list.

- Fear will keep you stuck in front of the TV watching others live the life that you're meant to live.

But fear is no more than a powerless scheme from a disempowered enemy. I say powerless because Psalms 2:4 says, "He Who sits in heaven laughs at the schemes of the enemy."

A few years ago, God gave me this great vision: I was walking along the path next to a beautiful river. This river was lined with trees and full of life in and around it, full of water activity. This river led to a sea. The sea wasn't the normal sea full of salt water that you would imagine. It was full of gems and riches. I could see rubies and diamonds and gems I had never seen before as well as gold and silver and riches I had never dreamed of. It was beautiful, and I had an innate sense that I/we were meant to enjoy it now. This was the abundance before us, the "heaven at hand" (see Matthew 3:2) for every child of God. As I walked toward the sea, I suddenly noticed a movement out of the corner of my eye. I turned to look and saw a tiny snake feverishly slithering back and forth in front of the abundance before my eyes. I thought to myself, "Ahhhhh, that's the enemy. Wow, he looks so small in comparison to all that God has for me." And in that moment, reality struck. The enemy really was minuscule compared to the goodness of God. He had pulled every trick in the book to keep me from the abundance, but that was just it— they really were just tricks, from a really tiny guy. That's why God could laugh. There was no substance to any of it unless I allowed there to be.

Whatever form the enemy takes in your life, that enemy has no authority. In addition, the power of God fueling your life is beyond anything that enemy can attempt to throw your way. An enemy has only the power we give it, period.

The Trick of Fear

Fear can only have a negative impact on your life when you allow it influence. Fear is nothing more than fear. It has no power over you except the power you give it. Fear is a type of belief. What you believe about something has a greater effect on your behavior and life than even the truth itself. Your beliefs directly affect your living. The beliefs in your mind directly affect your heart. Remember some of what we've previously learned in Chapter One; this is the beginning of a chain reaction:

- What you think affects what you believe.
- What you believe affects what you declare.
- What you declare affects how you behave.
- How you behave affects who you become.
- Who you become impacts your entire destiny.

You've most likely heard some version of this chain reaction before. As someone who has worked with people for nineteen years now, this is the chain reaction I see most often: Fear starts with a thought. Fear isn't a way of thinking; it's simply an emotion that started with a thought. When we linger or partner with that thought, the destruction begins. For example:

THOUGHT: "I saw an oil leak from the lawn tiller in the garage. What if something catches fire and my house explodes tonight?" (This is an actual thought I've had.)

DECLARATION: "Our house might blow up."

BEHAVIOR: Check and recheck the garage, which doesn't help the growing fear. Try to clean up the oil, which doesn't help the growing fear. Do research on the Internet about what can spark oil fires, which increases the fear . . . and the fear-based behaviors continue.

WHO I AM BECOMING: Someone who can't sleep. Someone plagued with fear. Someone who develops anxiety and possibly even physical ailments because of it.

MY DESTINY: I can't accomplish tasks because I'm tired. I can't take certain risks to carry out the plans for my life because of fear. I can't function at 100 percent because my body hurts.

This may sound extreme to you, but it's a very real chain reaction for many people. It's amazing when you open up with others about your own struggle with fear how much relatable fear is expressed in return. People hide their fears the way they hide an addiction. It's embarrassing for us to reveal to others what we're afraid of. The problem is, nothing can be dealt with in the dark. Until you bring something into the light, there is no hope for change. Light is meant to expose, but the fear of exposing ourselves is the first fear we have to face if we're to get healthy and become empowered to live in the level of faith that we desire.

Here's a possible common, everyday example of someone who thinks he or she doesn't actually have any struggles with fear:

> THOUGHT: I'm not good enough to get that dream job or promotion at work.

> DECLARATION: I'm pretty sure that (fill in the name) is going to get it instead. Besides, it probably would've been too hard for me anyway, and I bet I wouldn't even have enjoyed it.

> BEHAVIOR: The person doesn't apply for the dream job or go after the promotion.

> WHO THE PERSON BECOMES: Someone who doesn't take risks, who becomes resigned to "what if" scenarios and makes them reality.

> DESTINY: Is never achieved because fear keeps the person from going after it.

Wow. Ouch. This kind of fear-fueled scenario could be played out in the same way with relationships, kids, marriage, and most areas of life if we allow negative possibilities to dictate our reality. Negative thoughts, once agreed with, can keep us from pursuing an abundant life.

Fear is the cause of apathy. Apathy means to lose interest to the point of inaction. In every area of our lives, we're always doing one of two things: something or nothing. If there's an area in your life where you're doing nothing or that you feel apathetic about, you may want to examine whether fear is at the root of the problem. Sometimes our low levels of fear—even if we think we don't have a struggle with fear—keep us from the things we are destined for in life.

Remember Job? The book of Job in the Bible is the story of a man who lost everything, in spite of the fact that he loved and worshipped God. His life went pretty well south. That should make us feel afraid, right? After all, he still lost everything, even though he didn't have any bad thought patterns or beliefs.

Or did he?

Here is one secret of why Job possibly experienced what he did: "For the thing I greatly feared has come upon me, and what I dreaded has happened to me." (Job 3:25, New King James Version) Instead of living in a place of faith, he lived in fear and dread. Job outright declared that the destruction of his life was something he feared even before it happened. I said earlier that fear has only the power we give it. Is it possible that Job's partnering with fear created a magnet for destruction—and that it all started with fear-filled thoughts?

From Negative to Positive Chain Reaction

Thoughts of faith, on the other hand, can keep any accident, adversity, or tragedy from heading your way. Kris Vallotton, one of the Associate Leaders at Bethel Church in Redding, California, says, "Faith doesn't deny a problem's existence. It denies it a place of influence."

A unique and fascinating 2007 study on the effects of belief on cognitive performance by Carol Dweck, a psychologist at Stanford University, showed that children who believed that intelligence was malleable and could be improved were much more likely to perform well in school. Children who believed that intelligence was something set in stone—a genetic gift from birth that never changes—didn't perform as well.[1]

So what steps can we take to use the "chain reaction" to our benefit? Let's examine a more positive one:

- What God says affects what you think.
- What you think affects what you believe.
- What you believe affects what you declare.
- What you declare affects how you behave.
- How you behave affects who you become.
- Who you become impacts your entire destiny.

You'll notice that only one small but impactful change was made to this list—we started with what God says. We must allow that to influence the molecules of our existence.

The Water Experiment

Let's take a closer look at this "what we believe" chain reaction by noting science. In 2009, Dr. Masuro Emoto and his colleagues did an experiment on water.[2] They spoke over water, prayed over water, played music over water, and even placed labels on bottles of water with words that were meant to communicate to the water. After a documented period of time, the water was flash frozen and its molecular structure examined under a microscope. The first images below are of water samples taken from the Fujiwara Dam in Japan. Image 1 is the water

---

[1] Carol Dweck, "The Effect of Belief on Intelligence," *Mind Update,* December 27, 2007, http://www.mindupdate.com/2007/12/beliefs-about-intelligence-affect-cognitive-performance.

[2] Masaru Emoto, *The Hidden Messages in Water*, (Hillsboro, OR: Beyond Words Publishing, 2004).

before prayers were spoken over the water. Image 2 is the water after prayers spoken over the water. Dr. Emoto notes that even by simply observing the water with the natural eye, it looked clearer and more pristine. But when closely examined under a microscope, the results were astounding.

Image 1

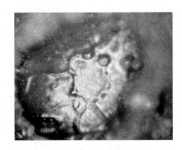

Image 2

Obviously this proves the power of declaration, but what does this have to do with thought?

Dr. Emoto took the experiment another step further. He and his colleagues placed labels over bottles of water where simple thoughts could only take place from one observing the bottle. The labels were meant to communicate with the water. The results were astounding similar. Image 3 below is water with the label "You make me sick. I want to kill you." Image 4 is from water with the label "Love and thanks."

Image 3

Image 4³

While this experiment itself is profound, it demands that we remember one very important fact about ourselves: Our human bodies are made up of more than 70 percent water. This means our words, our prayers, our thoughts, and our internal "labels" have power over our bodies. In this experiment is hard evidence of this truth.

As the New Testament says:

> "The tongue can bring death or life; those who love to *talk* will reap the consequences." (Proverbs 18:21, New Living Translation, emphasis added.)

> "And now, dear brothers and sisters, one final thing. Fix your *thoughts* on what is true, and honorable, and right, and pure, and lovely, and

---

³ All water images © Office Masaru Emoto, LLC

admirable. Think about things that are excellent and worthy of praise." (Philippians 4:8, New Living Translation, emphasis added.)

Belief in the Wrong Mindset

In Chapter One, I referenced a scripture that says "faith comes from hearing." (see Romans 10:17) Faith is simply belief in God's truth. Belief is one of the most powerful forces in the Bible—and in our lives. It is belief that awakens us to salvation:

> "For God so loved the world that He gave his only son. Whoever *believes* in Him will not perish but have eternal life." (John 3:16 emphasis add.)

It's not a duty that awakens us to salvation, or a set of rules, or an action we need to take. It is belief. It's belief that has aligned our hearts and minds with the heart of God. It's belief that awakens us to being a new creation. Belief opens our eyes to freedom.

Fear is rooted in a belief. Faith is rooted in a belief as well. Fear is the opposite of faith. Fear is the antithesis of faith. Fear and faith are in direct conflict with one another. Fear is belief in a wrong mindset.

FAITH...	FEAR...
Is the substance of things hoped for.	Is the substance of things not hoped for.
Is our awakening to salvation, freedom, and love.	Is a blinder.
Moves us toward our destiny.	Keeps us from our destiny.
Affects our brains positively.	Affects our brains negatively.

Faith and fear are not only tied to each other on opposite ends of the spectrum; they're also both directly related to how we view God. To me, this is why a correct understanding of the Fear of God is paramount. According to Christian psychiatrist, Timothy Jennings:

> Brain imaging has documented the phenomenon that, when we worship a vengeful God Who abuses freedom, when we anticipate the return of a punishing God, our fear circuits grow stronger and our prefrontal cortexes are damaged—again, in the brain region where we experience love, empathy and selflessness.[4]

> When we believe lies about God those false beliefs actually damage us, change our neural circuits, and warp our minds and characters. Conversely, when we receive the truth we are also changed, conformed back into the image of God through the working of His Spirit.[5]

> Brain research has demonstrated that the kind of God you worship changes your brain. Only the worship of the God of love brings healing. Holding to lies obstructs the healing process.[6]

Our beliefs are the lenses through which we view the world. Our beliefs affect how we think, which initiates either a negative or positive chain reaction. And everyone has beliefs. Even those who don't believe in God are placing belief in His nonexistence.

---

[4] Timothy R. Jennings, *The God-Shaped Brain*, (Downers Grove, IL: InterVarsity Press, 2013), 67.

[5] Ibid, 63.

[6] Ibid, 66.

Faith is not ignorance. It's a choice. It's a risk. It's a decision weighed by wisdom.

The following is a fascinating article that confirms the power of faith by Martin L. Rossman, contributing author for Healthy.net and founder of The Healing Mind company and web-resource center:

> When I was in my second year of practice, working in the county medical clinic, a middle-aged woman named Edna came in for a checkup. She was a likable, talkative person who said she had come because "the doctors worry me so and tell me I better keep an eye on my blood pressure." Her chart revealed that she had been diagnosed with a precancerous condition of the uterine cervix more than two years earlier, and the gynecologists she had seen wanted to take biopsies and remove the affected areas. Edna had turned this recommendation down four times, and each successive note put in her chart by her gynecologic consultants sounded more and more frustrated and concerned. There was mention of possible psycho-pathology and "irrational beliefs about healing."
>
> When I asked Edna why she was unnecessarily risking her life, she smiled broadly and told me that "Jesus will heal me, and I don't need surgery." She said she prayed and talked to Jesus every day, and He promised He would heal her if she put her trust in Him.
>
> I asked her how she communicated with Jesus, and she told me, "I see him when I pray, and he talks to me just like we're talking now." I again explained the medical concerns that I and the other doctors shared about her. Then I told her I had no doubt

that Jesus could heal her if He wanted to but that I wondered how long it would take. She was a bit surprised when I asked her if she would be willing to get in touch with Him and ask Him if He'd agree to heal her in the next six weeks.

She closed her eyes, and after a few minutes smiled and nodded her head. "Yes, He says He can and will heal me in six weeks." She agreed to have another pelvic exam and Pap smear at the end of six weeks and also agreed to have a cone biopsy performed if the Pap smear was still abnormal. "But it won't be," she said. "I know that now." And she left, smiling more widely than ever. I was glad to have obtained a commitment from her to have a biopsy if her prayer proved ineffective.

Six weeks later she returned. Her cervix looked normal on examination. Three days later her Pap smear report came back — perfectly normal. Edna's story certainly does not mean that you can forego Pap smears or that you must believe in Jesus. It does, however, point to the potent healing effects of faith and belief.[7]

He later continues with more confirmation of the power of faith:

The power of expectation and faith affects even surgical outcomes. In the 1950s there was a good deal of enthusiasm in the medical community about an operation that was quite successful in

---

[7] Martin L. Rossman, "Healing Power of the Mind - A Series by Martin Rossman, MD: Faith Healing, Placebo Effects, And Imagery," *Healthy.net*, http://www.healthy.net/Health/Article/Faith_Healing_Placebo_Effects_and _Imagery/8130.

relieving chest pain (angina pectoris) and improving heart function in men with blockage in their coronary arteries. The operation involved making an incision next to the breastbone and tying off a relatively superficial artery, which theoretically shunted more blood to the arteries supplying the heart. Most of the patients who underwent this procedure improved dramatically, experiencing both relief of pain and an improvement in heart function. Then a controlled study was done on the operation. A matched group of men with similar angina were brought to the operating room, they were anesthetized, and a surgical incision was made. Half of these men, however, were sewn up again without having anything else done. After surgery, they experienced the same dramatic relief of anginal pain and enjoyed the same improvement in heart muscle functioning as the men who underwent the real operation.[8]

After the in-depth study of fear on the brain, it is incredibly encouraging to hear about faith's effect, not only on the brain, but on the body as well. Faith is the currency of the supernatural. It pulls from the bank account that is already in our possession. Where faith exists, there is no room for fear.

Over and over again, Jesus' power is drawn out by the faith of others, as in these two stories in Mark 5:21-42 (New Living Translation, emphases added.):

> "Jesus got into the boat again and went back to the other side of the lake, where a large crowd gathered around Him on the shore. Then a leader of the

---

[8] Ibid.

local synagogue, whose name was Jairus, arrived. When he saw Jesus, he fell at His feet, pleading fervently with Him. "My little daughter is dying," he said. "Please come and lay Your hands on her; heal her so she can live." Jesus went with him, and all the people followed, crowding around Him.

A woman in the crowd had suffered for twelve years with constant bleeding. She had suffered a great deal from many doctors, and over the years she had spent everything she had to pay them, but she had gotten no better. In fact, she had gotten worse. She had heard about Jesus, so she came up behind Him through the crowd and touched His robe. For she thought to herself, "If I can just touch His robe, I will be healed." Immediately the bleeding stopped, and she could feel in her body that she had been healed of her terrible condition. Jesus realized at once that healing power had gone out from Him, so He turned around in the crowd and asked, "Who touched my robe?" His disciples said to Him, "Look at this crowd pressing around you. How can you ask, 'Who touched me?'" But he kept on looking around to see who had done it. Then the frightened woman, trembling at the realization of what had happened to her, came and fell to her knees in front of Him and told him what she had done. And He said to her, "Daughter, your *faith* has made you well. Go in peace. Your suffering is over."

While he was still speaking to her, messengers arrived from the home of Jairus, the leader of the synagogue. They told him, "Your daughter is dead. There's no use troubling the Teacher now." But Jesus overheard them and said to Jairus, "Don't be afraid. Just have *faith*." Then Jesus stopped the crowd and wouldn't let anyone go with him except Peter, James, and John (the brother of James). When they came to the home of the synagogue leader, Jesus saw much commotion and weeping and wailing. He went inside and asked, "Why all this commotion and weeping? The child isn't dead; she's only asleep." The crowd laughed at Him. But He made them all leave, and He took the girl's father and mother and his three disciples into the room where the girl was lying. Holding her hand, He said to her, "Talitha koum," which means "Little girl, get up!" And the girl, who was twelve years old, immediately stood up and walked around! They were overwhelmed and totally amazed."

How Does Faith in My Life Grow?

John Wimber, founder of the Vineyard church movement, once said, "Faith is spelled R-I-S-K." I've adopted this statement as one of my own now. The main hindrance to taking a risk is fear. And if you live controlled by fear, your faith will never grow. So an increase in faith happens by taking risk.

The first and greatest risk you can take is choosing intimacy with God. It's a risk not because He's scary, but because He is holy. "Holy" means set apart—something other than what we can understand. He is beyond our thoughts, understanding, and ways, and so He will encounter us beyond our thoughts, understanding, and ways. What else can you expect when the Creator of the Universe invades us little human beings? My husband, Rick, often says, "Sometimes the breakthrough you want is hidden inside an encounter that will make you uncomfortable." That's why it's called risk. Risk going deeper with God. Let Him show you new things, new revelations, new experiences, and new strategies for eliminating fear.

For example, consider these questions: If you want greater intimacy with your spouse, does it require risk-taking? Maybe in the area of communication? Maybe in the bedroom? Does it require risking your vulnerability? If you want to start your own business and be free of an employer, does it take risk?

Everything in life requires risk, even the bad things. You risk your health every time you overindulge in unhealthy eating habits. You risk not being able to pay the bills every time you impulsively spend too much money. You risk your liver when you get drunk. You risk your brain when you get high. You risk your relationships when you withdraw. You risk affection when you choose anger. So if we are going to take risks, we should take risks for the things we desire and not things that destroy.

REFLECTIONS

In this chapter, we learned that:

1. There is a chain reaction from belief to destiny at work in our lives. We can allow that chain reaction to have a positive effect in our lives by forming our beliefs based upon what God says.

Spend some time alone with God and ask Him what He says about your destiny. Write down His words.

_____

_____

_____

_____

_____

2. Fear is belief in the wrong mindset. Faith is belief in the mindset of God. Faith is the antithesis of fear and triggers forward motion toward our destiny.

What areas of your life do you want to see infused with faith?

_____

_____

_____

_____

3. Faith is spelled R-I-S-K.

What is the first step of risk you can take to infuse faith into the above-mentioned areas of your life?

_____

_____

_____

_____

_____

_____

CHAPTER SIX

Fear in the Church:
Recognizing Fear Bred in Churches

Power is of two kinds. One is obtained by the fear of punishment and the others by acts of love. Power based on love is a thousand times more effective and permanent than the one derived from fear of punishment.
Mahatma Gandhi

Church, as a location, should be the safest building you ever enter. Church, as a body of people, should be the safest family to join. Church, as an institution, should be the safest place to engage with.

Whoa! Wait! Stop! *What?!*

"Church—*safe?*" That's not my experience. And I'm guessing that my statements about church being "safe" have set off some alarms in your head as well.

As I move forward in this chapter, I am going to speak a lot about "the Church." The Church is everything I mentioned . . . a location or building, a body of people who believe in God, and an institution for spiritual growth. It encompasses all those descriptions. In addition, I realize the Church could refer to whatever is familiar for you, but as I'm speaking, I'm referring to my personal experiences in Evangelical & Charismatic Christianity.

Please don't misunderstand me, I do love the Church. Love. It. I believe that the potential of the Church is limitless for bringing power, life, and hope. But, currently and historically, the Church has not been considered safe by many. From the murderous Crusades of the Middle Ages to present-day judgmental picket lines against homosexuality, abortion, etc., the Church has developed an unsafe reputation.

Now, Jesus, on the other hand, is commonly seen as safe, even by those who see the Church as unsafe. Jesus offers transformation and unconditional love to everyone. Do the churches that tout His very name as their mantra operate with His character and love? In some ways, yes. And fortunately, the goal of many churches is to lead people to this Jesus. But on the whole, a lack of safety is a theme seen repeatedly in the Church. I will explain more as I continue.

Here are some examples of the lack of safety that I've witnessed in certain church circles:

- Anyone who lives a life that is labeled "unbiblical"—homosexuals, fornicators, pro-choice individuals, etc.—is judged, shunned, and unaccepted.

- Members who have "sin" uncovered are belittled, berated, and many times removed.

- Church leaders who have moral failures are made into spectacles, ridiculed, and shamed even if they're repentant and working towards personal growth.

- Many churches are not welcoming of those who believe in different doctrines or expressions of worship.

- Churches scare people into a relationship with God with threats of hell, punishment, and the wrath of God.

- The fear of God is more important than the love and grace of God.

- The Bible is used as a tool to punish people for their mistakes.

- There is an unspoken hierarchy of sins: The worse the sin, the more you'll be shunned.

This list breeds fear, not safety. Fear, unfortunately, is not only *in* the Church, but in many ways it is perpetuated *by* the Church. Church-bred fear causes people to hide their struggles when they walk in the doors. Fear actually thwarts the freedom we are searching for when we seek out church in the first place.

Denominational Divisions

I was raised in the Protestant denomination known as Independent Fundamental Baptists (IFB). My grandfather was one of the foremost leaders of this denomination. In the 1970s, *Time* magazine published an article about his church titled "Superchurch." At the height of its day, his church had more than 20,000 in attendance on any given Sunday. He helped to found the "megachurch" as we know it today. In many ways, I received a rich spiritual inheritance from his life.

But the IFB operated under its own interpretation of certain scriptures in the Bible that developed into a very rigid, strict doctrine. Women couldn't wear pants. Men couldn't have hair below their ears. Women could not be in any kind of leadership over men. Music must not have any kind of drum beat. These were only a few of the regulations I remember living by. This denomination imposed strict controls to keep sin at bay.

As a minister myself, I understand the temptation to use control as a way to deal with the fear that people in your church will "screw up." But control is a response to fear. Once a minister begins leading from a place of fear, love is left behind and falls farther and farther away.

Trying to live by a set of rules instead of by internal transformation can only be a temporary path, even for the leader of that path. My grandfather fell victim to his own set of rules under the IFB denomination. He fell into moral failure and violated his own standards—while simultaneously holding everyone around him accountable to the standards he was failing to live by. His ministry fell, books were written against him, and accounts of abuses committed by him and others in the IFB became public.

And because of the notorious shaming that happens when a leader falls, there was no place for my grandfather to come clean and deal with his own struggles. The Church that he had given his life for in many ways had taken his life from him.

Not everyone in the IFB, or any Christian denomination for that matter, is operating out of fear and control. Many amazing, loving people exist within all of these church walls. Every single church member is a beautiful creation of God with power and potential, including my grandfather. Here I am simply sharing an example of what happens when fear has its ugly rule.

My mother growing up in a church that operated in this way made the Church very unsafe for her. It took years of therapy to undo what her experiences in the Church had done. Isn't that ironic? For her, the place where healing should have thrived turned out to be the place where hope died.

How Has This Affected Me?

It sometimes surprises me that I'm in ministry myself. But I feel called to love the Church and everyone in it, even those who have given God and his Church a tarnished reputation. Because of my own struggle with fear, I believe I can relate to the destructive ramifications that fear can have in people's lives. All reason and sanity fly out the window when fear and control become our life tools.

Fortunately, I'm one generation removed from the direct pain in family. My parents moved me and my brother away from the ministry she grew up in when I was four years old. I'm forever grateful for the bold and scary move they took, because it allowed me to watch at a distance and not become blinded by a life I could have become entrenched in.

That's the funny thing about fear, isn't it? It becomes such a strong fabric woven into our emotional DNA that we don't even realize it's right there staring us in the face. We can't see that the decisions we make are based in fear. We can't see that the control we operate out of is based in fear. Fear becomes our security blanket because it deceives us into believing that we have some kind of control over our environment.

This type of control is common in the Church. Notice how, over the centuries, churches have moved away from being Jesus-focused to being sin-focused. Our sermons are focused on lust, greed, and pride instead of on Jesus, redemption, and grace. The reason this is ineffective is because *we become what we behold.* Whatever we focus on seeps into the depths of our hearts and desires. If we focus on sin, sin becomes what leads us, tempts us, and even controls our decisions. But focusing on the redemptive power of Jesus awakens us to be a people who live with a heart of redemption and mercy.

If you're on a diet and are trying to avoid ice cream, you may tell yourself, "I can't eat ice cream. I can't eat ice cream. I can't eat ice cream!...Why can't I stop thinking about ice cream?" Your very focus on the problem is keeping it right in front of your face and at the forefront of your mind. On the other hand, focusing on the solution makes the pathway to victory so much clearer.

As I've already mentioned earlier in the book, in 2 Corinthians, it says that by simply beholding the Lord, we're transformed into His image: "And we all, with unveiled face, beholding the glory of the Lord, are being transformed into the same image from one degree of glory to another. For this comes from the Lord who is the Spirit." (2 Corinthians 3:18, New American Standard Bible) Being transformed into His image includes not over-indulging in ice cream. It's not a process of striving. There is no need to be controlled. It's the focus on our God that causes everything else to fade away in His light. We go from victory to victory when we behold Him, not sin, around us.

As well-known blogger, Antwuan Malone, maintains:

> Sin is embarrassing, and embarrassment is definitely scary. But doesn't that make God's grace all the more impactful? Doesn't that help us appreciate the freedom found in God's forgiveness? Not a freedom to sin, mind you. Not even a freedom from conviction. But freedom to be fearless. Freedom to be open and without pretense. Freedom to love and be loved in the most natural way possible. No artificial flavoring. No preservatives.
>
> Too many people allow their fears to rob them of God's love, of even receiving the love of God's people. They walk into church with emotional flak jackets on and with arms firmly folded across their

bodies. Protected. They think from shame, I say from love. We've got to do something about that.[1]

Hurt people hurt people. Over the centuries, many people have been hurt by the Church. And those hurt in the Church begin to hurt others outside the Church. The two main hurts that I've seen occurring most commonly within the four walls of church are:

> The struggling church member who has become disillusioned because of the controlling, fear-instilling leader.

> The struggling leader who has been shunned by his church family for one failure.

Two Stories: Michelle and Mark

Michelle was a young girl who attended the same Christian school and church from preschool through second grade. She loved her school, church, friends, and teachers. One day, an unfortunate event occurred. Her mother discovered that Michelle's school principal was having an affair. His wife was a dear friend of Michelle's mother, so she immediately told the wife. In light of this discovery, Michelle's mother also confronted the principal.

In a culture of safety and honor, the principal would have felt he could come clean, repent, and find restoration within his church family. But he knew he couldn't. In fact, because he knew he would lose his job and everything he had if his failings were exposed, he expelled Michelle from the school instead. Michelle and her whole family were no longer allowed on the premises,

---

[1] Antwuan Malone, "I Am Afraid of Church…," *Candid Christianity*, November 29, 2010, http://antwuanmalone.com/afraid-the-church/.

and the principal did everything in his power to keep his actions from being revealed.

Michelle became disillusioned. She hopped from school to school almost every year from third grade through high school until she eventually dropped out of school. Church was no longer a place to find safety.

———

Mark had been in ministry since he was a teenager. He always helped out with youth groups, mission trips, and church services. He loved giving his time to the church. But Mark had a secret. He struggled with an addiction to pornography. Every time this addiction surfaced in Mark's life, he would try to hide it. He had seen in church that anyone who was experiencing a struggle like his would be ostracized by the circle of church friends and family. He had watched staff members get fired. He had witnessed backstabbing and gossip. So he hid. But his addiction grew until one day he was found out. Pornography was found on his work computer, and he was asked to resign. At this point, Mark was faced with a question: "Who can I trust?"

Mark had been attending a small church of loving believers and had become dear friends with the pastor, so he decided to take a risk and share with the pastor. Well, we can all guess what the result of that would be, right? But we would be wrong. The pastor wrapped his arms around Mark and said, "We're going to help you through this. We're going to love and support you. We want to help hold you accountable to your worth."

Over time, Mark was able to get completely free of his addiction because he was never judged, shamed, or discarded. He found a safe church that helped him focus on the love that would transform his life. Months later, he was invited to share his testimony with the entire church about the freedom that God had brought into his life. And that day, many others experienced breakthrough because of his story. Today, Mark serves full time in ministry.

The Difference

Michelle and Mark had very different experiences. Michelle experienced a church led by fear. She suffered in that environment, and so did her church's leadership. In that culture of fear, no one can grow, become healthy, find freedom, or experience real community. Her church became a façade of holiness operating out of a misunderstood fear of the Lord.

Mark, on the other hand, found a safe place in his church even though he had to take a risk to make that discovery. He could have been shunned and ended up still addicted today. Fortunately, his pastor had learned from the example of Jesus, Who extended grace and forgiveness in the midst of people's failures. Jesus didn't wait for people to come clean; He approached them with the goodness He could already see in their hearts. Then He extended grace to overcome their struggles, and they found love and forgiveness.

One of my favorite New Testament stories is that of the Samaritan woman at the well in John 4:1-42. Jesus approached her and asked her for water. In their exchange, He revealed to her that He knew that she had had several husbands and that she was not married to the man she was with at that point. She was shocked and waited for His condemnation. Instead, He revealed Himself as One who saves and redeems, and He explained what a true life of worship was to her. She ran back to Samaria to share the testimony of His grace and because of Jesus's redemptive approach to her life, many others in her city were transformed.

In my own life:

- I am moved by the way Jesus prophesied that His own disciple, Peter, would deny Him—but still gave him the keys to the foundation of the church. (see Matthew 16:13-20 and Matthew 26:30-35)

- I am challenged by Jesus' desire to dine in the home of Zaccheus, the tax collector, and extend value for this man in the midst of Zaccheus' shrewdness. (see Luke 19:1-10)

- I am undone by Jesus' defense of the prostitute when He drew a line in the sand and declared to her accusers, "He who is without sin casts the first stone." His powerful action and simple words to "go and sin no more" changed her life forever. (see John 8:1-11)

- I am convicted by Jesus' desire to touch the demon-oppressed, mentally ill, and severely diseased with no fear of becoming unclean Himself. He was moved by compassion to see others set free, and He knew that love was the only cure.

Love is the only cure.

It is the cure for injustice. It is the cure for sin. It is the cure for depravity, disease, and depression. Love should be running through the veins of the body of Christ and be our mantra unto the world . . . and unto our own church families.

Love casts out fear—all fear:

"There is no fear in love, but perfect love casts out fear. For fear has to do with punishment, and whoever fears has not been perfected in love." (1 John 4:18)

What Is the Church's Reputation in Society?

A number of recent studies, articles, and polls have shown that Americans are losing interest in churches as institutions. For example, as author and religious commentator Steve McSwain, known as "the voice for the SBNR (Spiritual But Not Religious)," has observed:

> Clearly, the Church is dying. According to the Hartford Institute of Religion Research, more than 40 percent of Americans "say" they go to church weekly. As it turns out, however, less than 20 percent are actually in church. In other words, more than 80 percent of Americans are finding more fulfilling things to do on weekends.
>
> Between the years 2010 and 2012, more than half of all churches in America added not one new member. Each year, nearly 3 million more previous churchgoers enter the ranks of the religiously unaffiliated.
>
> However, people are still interested in spirituality. In fact, the phrase "spiritual but not religious" has become its own religion. People who claim this title are "SBNRs." They hunger after the transcendent and supernatural. They want a spiritual experience that brings wholeness and growth, not a judg-

mental experience that brings them condemnation and fear.[2]

However, did you know that *even God* is not in the business of judging? "The Father judges no one, but has given all judgment to the Son." (John 5:22) And Jesus, the Son, has an answer to that verse: "You judge according to the flesh; I judge no one." (John 8:15)

And yet, many feel that the Church has appointed itself both judge and jury of the world. The harsh stance of many churches toward those who are different from them leads people away from Jesus—not toward Him. In fact, the only people Jesus ever had harsh words for were those who did the judging, the religious crowd. His words were not for the sinner, but for the "religious elite" who failed to recognize their own sin.

The Church has no business judging—we've been given the ministry of reconciliation! It's our mission to show the love of God and to reconcile others' minds back to the truth of Who God is and how He feels about them:

> "All this is from God, Who through Christ reconciled us to Himself and gave us the ministry of reconciliation; that is, in Christ God was reconciling the world to Himself, not counting their trespasses against them, and entrusting to us the message of reconciliation." (2 Corinthians 5:18-19)

Along these lines, one of the most interesting stories in the Bible is told in Mark 8. Jesus had just fed a crowd of 4,000 with seven

---

[2] Steve McSwain, "Why Nobody Wants to Go to Church Anymore," *Huffington Post*, October 14, 2013, http://www.huffingtonpost.com/steve-mcswain/why-nobody-wants-to-go-to_b_4086016.html.

loaves. Shortly after, He was questioned by the "religious" who seemed to ignore this grand miracle and instead asked Him for a sign to test who He said He was. Once he was alone with His disciples, the ones closest to Him, their issues became clear. The disciples, forgetting the miracle that had just occurred, became concerned because they had not brought bread with them for the journey. But Jesus, instead of addressing the physical matter of no bread, jumped straight to the spiritual matter at hand: "And He cautioned them, saying, 'Watch out; beware of the leaven of the Pharisees and the leaven of Herod.'" (Mark 8:15)

The Pharisees represented a controlling religious system, and Herod represented a controlling political system. It was clear from the disciples' concerns that the Pharisees' doubts had seeped into their own minds. The Pharisees could not see Jesus for who He was, even though He had just demonstrated His power with a grand miracle. The disciples then allowed the Pharisees' thinking to affect their own—which Jesus promptly pointed out to them. A little bit of self-righteous religion leavens the whole bunch. Self-righteous religion carries such subtle deception that it disguises itself as sensible logic. Unfortunately, it is law-based, rule-based, and sin-based – and it requires fear and control.

My Dream

About five years ago, I had a dream that had a great impact on my life. In this dream, I was standing on the balcony of an apartment building with my mother. This apartment building had a strange design. It had odd angles, balconies jutting out in various directions, and a design that looked unstable. But we could see that it had a large, wide, solid foundation beneath it. We were looking at another apartment building across the street. It was tall, narrow, and traditional. It had no balconies and a straightforward design. It was beige in color. It looked solid enough in its rectangular stature, but it was built on a foundation that was as narrow as the building it supported.

Suddenly a strong wind began to blow. My mom and I watched from our balcony as the other apartment building began to sway in the wind. As the wind blew harder, the building began to bend. Suddenly it snapped in half, and people began falling from its windows to the ground below and into a large pool. But this pool was not saving them. Many of them were struggling for life as they hit the water.

I felt called to make my way to the pool as quickly as possible. I ran out of my building and across the street to the pool. God was highlighting the people I was supposed to save. I jumped in and began pulling those people out and setting them on the path to the building I had come from. The even stranger part of the dream was I knew certain people in the pool were clearly not going to make it, and I had to "finish them off" (sounds harsh but I'll be clearer in the revelation).

When I woke up from this dream, I began to pray about it and had multiple revelations. The apartment building I was in was the Church as it was meant to be designed, with various facets and unique designs coming together in one building that worked together and stood on one strong foundation. The apartment building that fell was the narrow-minded, judging version of the Church. When hit with the wind of God's Spirit, it cracked and fell. It could not withstand the power of God's Spirit. The Holy Spirit had revealed the hearts of those who could find freedom and those who are determined to lead from a place of religious control. Those two groups were the ones highlighted. I felt moved to save those who were willing to get free and reveal those caught in a negative religious mindset.

I later had a conversation with David Moore, a friend of ours who has been a pastor for more than thirty years. I asked him, "How do you think we should treat the self-righteous religious?

112

They were the one group of people that Jesus actually called names and expressed anger toward. Does that give us permission to do the same?" David explained with wisdom that there's a difference between those who have fallen prey to the deceptions of a negative religious system and those who actually represent the negative religious system itself. Jesus's harsh words were for those who represented and perpetuated that system, not for those who were its victims. It reminded me of the two types of people I had encountered in the pool in my dream.

There's no room for a controlling, fear-based religious system that keeps people bound up in fear. It is not what Jesus died for.

Grace Is Beyond Sin

One thing I've learned about fear is that it's usually irrational. When irrationality enters the picture, we begin to create rules around things that are of no consequence, for example:

- We move from rules about modesty to deciding that women can't wear pants.
- We move from rules on drunkenness to prohibiting all alcohol.
- We move from rules regarding order to limiting freedom in worship.

These "rules" only scratch the surface of some of the irrational regulations I've encountered in the Church. No wonder people don't want to go to church anymore.

Can we change things? Can we create an environment of freedom without fear? It's tricky. But it's possible with a certain element that makes anything possible: Grace.

Grace makes us righteous. Justice is fulfilled through grace:

"But now the righteousness of God has been manifested apart from the law, although the Law and the Prophets bear witness to it—the righteousness of God through faith in Jesus Christ for all who believe. For there is no distinction: for all have sinned and fall short of the glory of God, and *are justified by His grace as a gift*, through the redemption that is in Christ Jesus, whom God put forward as a propitiation by his blood, to be received by faith. This was to show God's righteousness, because in His divine forbearance He had passed over former sins. It was to show His righteousness at the present time, so that He might be just and the justifier of the one who has faith in Jesus." (Romans 3:21-26, emphasis added)

How is it possible that we can be made righteous through no effort of our own—so much so that for us to try to attain our own righteousness would be to say that what Jesus did in giving His life was not enough? "For our sake He made Him to be sin who knew no sin, so that in Him we might become the righteousness of God." (2 Corinthians 5:21)

And grace is for everyone, not just some:

"Therefore, just as sin came into the world through one man, and death through sin, and so death spread to all men because all sinned—for sin indeed was in the world before the law was given, but sin is not counted where there is no law. Yet death reigned from Adam to Moses, even over those whose sinning was not like the transgression of Adam, who was a type of the one who was to come. But the free gift is not like the trespass. For if many died through one man's trespass, much more have the grace of God and the free gift by the grace of that one man Jesus Christ abounded for many. And the free gift is not like the result of that one man's sin. For the judgment following one trespass brought condemnation, but the free gift following many trespasses brought justification. For if, because of one man's trespass, death reigned through that one man, much more will those who receive the abundance of grace and the free gift of righteousness reign in life through the one man Jesus Christ." (Romans 5:12-17)

This removes all room for judgment on our part. Grace allows Jesus to trade places with us. Grace obtains for us what Jesus deserved because He took what we deserved. We talk so much about the power of Jesus to save, to heal, to deliver. But what about His substitutionary power, the power to take our place? He died the death we were supposed to have to die. He killed sin, so sin wouldn't kill us.

"Grace" is evidence that *Jesus* did it.

But aren't I supposed to be working out my own salvation? With fear and trembling?

"Therefore, my beloved, as you have always obeyed, so now, not only as in My presence but much more in My absence, *work out your own salvation with fear and trembling,* for it is God Who *works* in you, both to will and to work for His good pleasure." (Philippians 2:12-13, emphasis added)

Let's take a moment to examine this scripture and see if Jesus' part ended at our death, burial and resurrection in Jesus. Let's see if we're supposed to take over at this point and work out this gift of salvation. In these verses, there are two forms of the word "work": "*work* out your own salvation with fear and trembling" and "for it is God Who *works* in you."

The first use of "work" is *katergazomai* in the Greek. It literally means "to perform or achieve." The second use of "work" is *energeo* in the Greek, which means "to put forth power or to be operative." Reading these verses back to back, we see that if we "perform" or try to "achieve" our own salvation, we should do it with fear and trembling. Why? Because we aren't the ones who operate the power in our salvation at all—it's God—God Who brings power to our lives.

We have to understand the true meaning of scriptures as well as reading them in context with the whole word of God. Here's my reworking of Philippians 2:12-13: "If you're going to work out your own salvation, do it with fear and trembling, because it's not you who should be doing it—it's God."

Living In a World of Grace

What is it like to live in a world of grace? It's messier than in a world of rules, because it introduces freedom. When you aren't trying to control people, you give them an opportunity to make their own choices. When people make their own choices, sometimes they make messes. But when they make messes, they learn how to clean them up. And when they learn how to clean them up, they mature.

Grace reveals that Jesus in *us* can be trusted. Grace is not mercy. Grace is the empowerment of the individual. Grace says, "Jesus did it all for you, and I'm going to believe Him to be powerful enough to reveal transformation in you."

That doesn't mean we don't confront people or we don't help them to see the messes they've made. What it does mean is that we don't control people or hold them up to a set of standards that *we* design. Rather, we show them Jesus as the Standard, knowing that by beholding Him, they will be transformed into His image (see 2 Corinthians 3:18).

Grace facilitates the development of an environment of freedom within which people can take risks because they're free to fail. Grace allows people to be who they are without living under the pressure of comparison. Grace makes room for the unique aspect of God's glory in each one of us to shine. Grace reminds me, "I am powerful. I am beautiful. I am special."

Lastly, grace makes church a safe place once again. We no longer have to find our identity in our choices, our jobs, our appearances, or our history. Our identity is tied to the One who released empowering grace in our lives. As we give ourselves to His grace, we find that we're more than capable of living out the destiny of our dreams. And as we live by His grace, we find that we're able to see others with the glory that God created in them so that they, too, can live out their destinies.

REFLECTIONS

In this chapter, we have learned that:

1. We become what we behold. If we focus on sin as *the* issue in church, it will only breed more sin. If we focus on Jesus, we will be transformed into the image of the One Who already took care of sin.

List some of the issues in your life that feel impossible to overcome.

_____

_____

_____

_____

_____

_____

2. Fear and control in the Church are ineffective tools for personal transformation. Creating a culture of grace is the answer to making an unsafe church environment safe once again.

Spend some alone time with God and ask Him to show you what the issues above would look like when grace and restoration are applied.

CHAPTER SEVEN

"Just When I Thought It Was Over": Facing Panic Attacks and Physical Anxiety

Rick and I were heading down a back road to visit some friends. It was only six o'clock in the evening, but it was already dark out as it was right in the middle of December. Rick was sharing about his day, the news he had read, and the appointments he'd had when I suddenly became very aware of how dark this back road was. I noticed that there were no streetlights. I glanced down at the GPS, and it said we still had fourteen more miles to go on this road. And then everything changed in a way that I never expected it to. My heart began to race. My palms began to sweat. My body began to shake. And my mind—oh, my overwhelmed mind—was bombarded with fears of the unknown! "What if we get trapped out here? What if the car breaks down? What if I get sick? What if a tire blows?"

Then it got worse. We suddenly came to a complete stop because we had reached a set of railroad tracks and the barrier was down. As the train passed and the seconds ticked by, my panic increased, and my body reacted as it never had before. I felt as if I was either going to pass out or explode with adrenaline and jump out of the car. All I could think was, "What if this train derails and hits us?!" I couldn't shake that thought. The few minutes Rick and I sat there felt like hours.

When the train was gone and we were moving again, I burst into tears. "I don't know what's wrong with me," I sobbed to Rick. "Why am I feeling this way? What's happening in my body?" I told him what I was experiencing and that I didn't think I could move forward with our dinner plans that evening, but we did. I made him promise that we would take the freeway home, not the back roads.

What Changed In That Moment?

As I've shared with you throughout these pages, I've felt my fair share of fear. But all my life, I've been able to fight off the thoughts eventually and get on with life. Even though thoughts recurred and fears continued to push against me, I've always been strong enough to regain my footing and not let them keep me from my pursuits.

But I had never had a physical panic attack in response to fear until that evening, and it happened while we were driving on a back road to someone's house—something I had done more than a hundred times in my life with no problems or even a second thought. But now real fear had set in. Something seemed wrong in my brain, and the manifestation of fear in my body was confirming that suspicion.

Over the weeks and months that followed, I experienced what I imagine mental illness feels like. I didn't want to drive anywhere because we might get caught in traffic and I'd be trapped and have a panic attack. I looked for reasons to get out of dinners and appointments with friends because I might have a panic attack in their presence. I didn't want to go to the mall because the crowds might give me a panic attack. I couldn't even think about flying in an airplane, riding a train, or being in the backseat of a car without breaking into a cold sweat. I was inundated with the craziest and most irrational fears I'd ever had in my life— that a bomber might walk into Starbucks and blow us up, or that the guy next to me in line might have a gun, or that if I went anywhere, I could get trapped. Trapped in a store, trapped in a line, or trapped at the bank.

I'm not exaggerating. Fortunately, I had already been in counseling for a year when the panic attacks began. I was not in counseling for fear, though. I was going to counseling to deal with my past. I thought I had already dealt with fear. I thought I had victory in my life. I'd had revelations given to me about the Fear of the Lord and living life with wisdom. I lived out daily practices in my life that propelled me to take risks and go after my dreams. I had made myself the poster child for "No Fear." Right? Apparently not.

Just when I thought it was over, a whole new and more intense engagement with fear had begun.

I needed help. After a couple of weeks of this incessantly irritating way of living, I knew I must not become that person. I could not live trapped in fear. I had a great destiny in front of me.

So I began to share what was happening with my counselor, Otis. He had heard the stories of my childhood and young adult life. They weren't the happiest stories, but he told me repeatedly that I was a strong person and that inside me was a strong girl who had been taking care of me through the ups and downs of my emotional life. But one day we both realized this strong girl was tired. There were things in my past that this strong girl could not hold in any longer. That's why the panic attacks had begun.

One day, I told him about one memory in which all I could remember was myself screaming. All I could see was a white hallway. That's what I had to work with. I knew I had experienced a lot of medical issues as an infant and all the way through the age of ten—hospitalizations, surgeries, tests and spinal taps. I didn't remember most of it, but that day, in Otis's office, I did remember something: screaming. Lots of screaming.

Otis began guiding me back to places in my childhood that I had never connected with. Small pieces began coming to me. Many memories were of the hospital, while others were of being trapped in a full-leg cast for my entire first year of life. But the true beginning of the breakthrough for me was when I went back and saw myself in the womb.

My parents were in a near-fatal car accident while my mom was pregnant with me. She was a little over halfway through the pregnancy, so the accident was a dangerous event. They survived unharmed, but my mom suffered from excruciating pain under her ribs for the rest of the time she carried me. The doctors believed that my foot had become caught under her ribs.

That theory was confirmed when I was born. My mom labored for thirty-six hours with no epidural, and her water had already broken. She was fully dilated, but my little body had not dropped one inch. I was stuck. My mom began running a fever, and infection was inevitable if they didn't deliver me quickly. She was rushed in for an emergency cesarean section and, thankfully, I was born a healthy nine pounds and six ounces. Except for one thing: my right foot.

Because it had been caught under my mom's ribs, it had developed facing backwards and upside down. The only term they had for my condition was "clubfoot," but it was more severe than that. I was placed in a cast as an infant. The doctors kept putting casts on me that covered more and more of my body, because I always found a way to scramble out of them. The cast eventually had to be made large enough to keep me immobilized so my foot could be reshaped. After one year in the cast, at the age of one, I had my first surgery.

What I came to remember about being in the womb was the feeling of being trapped. And as I remembered, I began to have a panic attack in Otis's office. I had felt trapped as a fetus. I had felt trapped as an infant in those casts. I had felt trapped going into all my surgeries. I had felt trapped being subjected to invasive tests and procedures. I had felt trapped being cared for intravenously when my fever would spike to 107 or 108 degrees. I had felt trapped being fed through a tube down my nose. I had felt trapped in painful correcting boots and physical therapy. I had felt trapped in the hands of another human being because, in my mind, pain was the inevitable result.

It was this child who came back to life inside me that day. This child, afraid of being trapped. This child, afraid of people. This child, afraid of life. This child could not be strong any longer.

In Otis' office that day, I asked myself, "What was I in for now? What was I going to do?"

There Is Jesus

Otis uses a method of connecting his patients to Jesus in their memories. As I began to foggily wade through some of my memories, Otis always brought me to Jesus. Jesus had always been there, loving that scared little girl. And Jesus was still here, loving this scared big girl.

I clearly remember the breakthrough that came from that session with Otis. I had asked Rick to come with me. I didn't think I could handle the barrage of panic attacks anymore. I needed support. I needed my husband with me. Something about his presence helped me feel safe to dig a little deeper.

As Otis guided me to memories in the womb, fear got stronger. Every time I had to picture myself there, I began to panic. Most of the time, I wanted to run to the bathroom and throw up. I didn't want to stay there. I wanted to leave the memory. This time, though, I pressed on. As I pressed on, I could see my own pain. It broke my heart. I could feel the compassion of Jesus in me—for me. I saw this baby girl delivered by C-section. And then, clear as day, I saw her foot, mangled and deformed, in front of me. I immediately began sobbing. I had never seen it before. I had grown up being told what it looked like, but I couldn't remember it myself because I was just an infant—a newborn. But in this memory, God showed it to me. I could see how desperately I needed the cast and the surgeries. I could understand that I had been trapped. I could accept that I'd had to go through pain and discomfort to correct my foot. I could look back as an adult and accept why this unknowing baby had had to endure the hospitalizations. This revelation brought me freedom.

Revelation is a key to freedom from fear.

The revelation of Jesus being there for me brought freedom. The revelation of the reality of my physical condition brought freedom. The revelation of God's protection in the womb brought freedom. The revelation of Jesus still here for me facing my past brings freedom. These revelations are what have freed me from many of my fears.

Revelations made overcoming fear possible for me. And knowing that there are more revelations to receive allows me to face other fears. Allow the revelation of Jesus to bring you freedom today in the areas you've been afraid to face.

Revelation & Wisdom

Revelation leads to wisdom.

I've talked very frankly about the need to hear the voice of God in our lives. His voice is our direction for what we declare and think. But His voice goes much deeper than words. His voice carries revelation with it—every time. Our God is so magnificent that every word carries the richness of 10,000 words. Every phrase has revelation to unpack. Every sweet sentence is like a gold mine. And what do you do in a gold mine? You mine.

Which means that beyond hearing God's voice, it's valuable to steward what He says. Stewardship isn't a principle of management. We don't want to just manage what we've been given. If you start out with $100, you don't want to just manage that $100 so you still have only $100 ten years from now. You want to steward that $100 for increase so you'll have $100,000 in ten years.

Every time God speaks, we are given a wealth of wisdom to mine for our lives. His every conversation with us offers us revelation about His character, His heart, and His love. Let's examine this truth on a practical level.

When my husband and I have a conversation, his language communicates something about him every time he speaks. His body language communicates that he longs for physical touch. His words communicate that he enjoys gaining knowledge and understanding. His eyes speak that he is a person full of joy. His laugh speaks of his optimistic outlook. His tears speak of his compassion. His stride speaks of his integrity. Every way that he communicates reveals something about his heart and his character. The level to which I mine what he's revealing to me is the level to which I allow him to have an impact on my life. The same is true about God.

Think about the amazing messages you've heard. Think about the powerful books you've read. Think about the prophetic words you've received. Think about the intimate times God has spoken His heart to you. How many of those moments of revelation have you mined and assimilated into your life? How many of those messages from God are a part of how you live today? Or are they forgotten? Does He continue to repeat Himself?

How frustrating is it when you tell someone something and have to repeat it again and again, especially when you're sharing your heart for that person. If I respond with fear and mistrust when Rick tells me he loves me, I miss out on the deeper connection he's offering me.

God wants us to see His heart. When Jesus said to pray "Your kingdom come, Your will be done, on earth as it is in heaven" (see Matthew 6:10), it wasn't a tease. "Your kingdom" is God's kingdom. Jesus wouldn't tell us that we could pray for earth to look like heaven if it wasn't reality. God wants to reveal to us the revelation in His kingdom. Not only does He want to—He does.

Sometimes it's not another word from God that we need. Sometimes we need to mine the words of the past for our lives today. Many times we may feel that He isn't speaking to us. You may wonder, "Why don't I hear him?" But maybe He has already spoken, and what would actually help is to mine what He has said.

Why is it so important to mine the revelation within the word that God has given you? Because revelation is the seed of wisdom. Wisdom, not fear, is the key to decision making. Inside every single acorn of revelation is a giant oak tree of wisdom.

Let's look at one story of the Apostle Paul. In Acts 9, when Paul was still called Saul, he was blinded on the road to Damascus and spoken to by Jesus. As he waited to regain his sight, a man named Ananias (not the same Ananias with Sapphira) was instructed to find Saul and give him this message: "So Ananias departed and entered the house. And laying his hands on him he said, 'Brother Saul, the Lord Jesus Who appeared to you on the road by which you came has sent me so that you may *regain* your sight and be *filled* with the Holy Spirit.'" (Acts 9:17, emphasis added)

"Regain your sight and be filled with the Holy Spirit." There is a depth of revelation in this message from God. "Regain" in the Greek actually means to recover, and "recover" implies that something has been lost. Obviously Saul's physical sight had been lost, but so had his spiritual sight. Saul had been created in the image of God but had become a man who spent his life persecuting God. Once his sight was regained, he could see everything clearly. His recovery was so radical that he became one of the disciples he had once persecuted.

As far as the second part, being filled with the Holy Spirit, Saul's encounter was so powerful that he received a name change because of it. When Saul became Paul, he began to operate as the father of the Holy Spirit's movement in all of the churches in the Middle East. He was not only filled with the Holy Spirit—he also mined the revelation that being "filled" means to be "filled to overflowing." He spilled out the same power he had received to every life he influenced. There was so much activity of the Holy Spirit going on all around him that he had to be consulted by many of the burgeoning churches about how to manage it. Paul ended up writing two-thirds of the New Testament.

If Paul had simply received the message "Regain your sight and be filled with the Holy Spirit" and taken it at face value, our Christian history may not look the way it does today. An oak tree of wisdom was developed through his mining of that first word he received from God.

You can imagine him going into the church of the Corinthians and asking himself, "How can I help these people regain their sight and be filled with the Holy Spirit?" He probably evaluated himself by thinking, "How can I operate with clear sight regarding how God sees these people and walk in my fullness of the Holy Spirit in their presence?" Do you see the richness in this phrasing?

Now imagine the revelation to be discovered in the words that God has given you. In fact, don't just imagine it, go find it! It's there. There's so much wisdom for living a life free from fear and full of faith in what God has already said.

God once said to me about a particular circumstance I was facing, "What you *believe* affects your behavior more than the truth itself." For example, if I believed that someone was a liar, even if they were telling me the truth, I would still not extend them trust. The revelation that what you believe affects your behavior more than the truth itself has been something I've contemplated and mined again and again. As a person who has struggled with trust issues and fears of abandonment and being lied to, I've chosen to mine the gold in this revelation. I've learned to examine my beliefs and how I'm allowing those beliefs to affect my behavior. I look for the truth of God's word to motivate my behavior. In fact, I've mined that one revelation so deeply for wisdom that it's had a great impact on much of what I speak about and on what I've written in this book.

Water Your Oak Tree with Faith

Here's how we can apply faith, as discussed in Chapter Four. When we receive revelation and mine it for wisdom, we still want to see this wisdom working in our daily lives. We get comfortable with our old way of thinking, so we have faith that this new way will work. We renew our minds.

Here is a great description of what well-known blogger, Brandon Pahhty, describes as "the blueprint of renewing your mind":

> Imagine that you've lived at your house for 20 years.

You've memorized the fastest ways to drive home from your work, from church, from your friend's place, from school, and from the gym. You've developed a route that you take every time. You don't think about it; that's just the way you go home because you've done it that way for twenty years. You know the correct turns to make. You know the best time to take which route based on how bad traffic is. You know which roads have the most cops. And you know all the ins and outs of getting yourself home.

Then imagine you move ten minutes away.

The next day, you're about to head back home from work. You get in your car as usual, and you start driving. Out of sheer habit and muscle memory, you take the same old highway and the same old exit all the way until you get home, only to realize that you no longer live at your old house. You slap yourself on the forehead, thinking, "How could I forget?! I moved! Gotta make sure I don't do this again...what a waste of time!"

The next day is similar; you get into your car and you begin to take the same route you've taken for the last 20 years. It isn't until about halfway home you realize again, "Shoot! I moved!" You pull a U-turn and head towards the new home.

So by this point, you're consciously making an effort to make sure it doesn't happen again. You create a reminder in your head, "When I reach this street, I have to make a left where I used to make a right." You know it will take a conscious effort to forge a new pattern because the old pattern was so familiar, natural, and comfortable. But you know you have to do it because you no longer live at the old house—none of your belongings are there. Plus, the new house is much bigger, with a lot more freedom to move around.

The next day, as you leave your house for work, you make another mental note to remind yourself that you've moved so that you won't forget at the end of the day. The time arrives, and you get into your car. Confident, reminding yourself that you have a new home, you get all the way home without taking a wrong turn. When you arrive, you breathe a sigh of satisfaction, knowing that you took the right route and you're confident it'll be easier next time.

Over a period of a few weeks, what started with lots of errors and mistakes starts to become second nature and natural. The muscle memory and old pattern of thinking was undone, and now it's hard to imagine ever taking that old route again. In addition to that, you've done the same exercise with your church, school, friend's place, and the gym. You've reprogrammed and redesigned your routes to fit the location of your new home.

Months down the road, it's nowhere near a struggle. You've forged a new routine—a new habit. You arrive at your new home every time. And every once in a while, you'll be at an intersection you used to use when you were at your old house and you'll get a flashback to when you used to slam the pedal to try to make the light. You may even reminisce on the memories. But then you snap back into reality, remembering, "Well, I don't live there anymore."

This is our life. This is the call of Romans 12:2 to "renew your mind." As a believer, you have a responsibility to renew your thinking, to rewire your brain as a result of understanding the facts that you are a child of God and you have been given a new nature (new tendencies). Renewing your mind should cause you to make different choices. It is a different path—a different life than you once lived.

The old house had its own set of ways and its own set of patterns. If we find ourselves veering off onto old paths, it's only because we've forgotten that we've moved to a new house that's more glorious.[1]

I love this analogy! Every time I choose the path to my new house, I'm rewiring my brain to wisdom.

Plant that seed of revelation, water it with faith, and watch it grow into a mighty oak tree of wisdom:

> "He will be like a tree firmly planted by streams of water, which yields its fruit in its season and its leaf does not wither; and in whatever he does, he prospers." (Psalm 1:3)

> "They will be called oaks of righteousness, a planting of the Lord for the display of his splendor." (Isaiah 61:3b)

---

[1] Brandon Pahhty, "The Blueprint of Renewing Your Mind," *I Am A Spirit...Jesus*, November 27, 2011, http://www.iamaspirit.org/archives/2438.

REFLECTIONS

In this chapter, we have learned that:

1. Jesus was there in every event of our past. Getting in touch with His heart in those events is paramount to discovering our freedom from fear.

Spend some time alone with God and ask Him to show you some memories that still create fear in your present.

_____

_____

_____

_____

_____

_____

2. The revelation of God's heart for us carries a gold mine of wisdom for us to steward.

Write down some of the promises or prophetic words you have received in your life.

_____

_____

_____

_____

_____

3. Pick one promise or word from above and begin to mine it for wisdom in your life.

Write down what God reveals.

_____

_____

_____

_____

_____

_____

CHAPTER EIGHT

The Haunting:
Releasing the Fears of Our Past

John and Mary are newly married and enjoying the sweetness of their long-awaited union. John works hard at the local county government office preparing paperwork for new tax laws. Mary stays at home developing a home-based business for marketing consulting. They love their new life together, and so far marriage feels easy and natural.

One Tuesday evening, Mary is preparing dinner for John. She sets the table, finishes the trimmings for the roast, and sits down to wait for his arrival. After some time passes, she looks at her watch and sees that he's fifteen minutes late. While most women would take a moment to process and understand the possible reasons for their husband's tardiness, Mary doesn't. Immediately, her mind flashes back to a previous relationship that was full of lies, deceit, and infidelity. She begins imagining John with another woman, trying to quickly wrap up his rendezvous before coming home to Mary.

Mary has succumbed to fear, which is creating additional emotions of anger, insecurity, and distrust. Her heart is racing, her blood is boiling, and she's already allowing the images that fear has created in her mind to dictate thoughts of ending her marriage. By the time John walks through the door, he's seventeen minutes late. Instantly, he sees that Mary isn't her usual welcoming self. So he reaches for her lovingly, but she moves away and responds coolly with, "Where have you been?"

Taken aback by the harshness in her voice, John glances at the clock and sees that it is only 6:17 p.m. Normally he aims to be home by 6 p.m., so he isn't that late. He decides to extend grace to his wife anyway.

"I was trying to send an urgent fax to the state office," he explains, "but the line was busy for fifteen minutes."

While Mary can hear the logic in what John's saying, she realizes that fear is still whispering lies of doubt to her heart—and she breaks down in tears at this realization.

That night, Mary realizes something—her past is still haunting her.

A Familiar Story

Does this too-familiar story resonate with you? It does with me. The past may still be dictating our fear in the present and fear of the future. I have a keen understanding of the effects our pasts can have on us, and I'm still pursuing complete victory over some areas of my own past. I believe that every human being can relate to something in their past haunting them.

Whenever we're confronted with an echo of our past, whether it's a familiar situation, a familiar feeling, or a familiar person, familiarity reaches back into the previous years of life and pulls them into the present day to haunt us, whether for good or bad. Why do I still want to go to Magic Mountain and ride roller coasters? Because it brings back the familiar feeling of joy I always experienced there as a child. Why do I avoid going to the doctor? Because of all the years I spent hospitalized as a child. The feeling of despair from those memories overwhelms me.

Every experience in life creates a memory that leaves an imprint on us, emotionally and physically. New research has begun to reveal that we have cellular memory. So while many of us want to believe we've done everything we possibly can—counseling, coaching, etc.—to move on from past experiences, only God sets us free. Remember that nothing is impossible for God, including freeing us from our past. Our belief in that truth will lead to more freedom from our past than we have ever experienced.

Where Is Jesus?

If you're not a believer in Jesus, this section may not be completely clear to you, but it can still apply if you keep an open mind and heart. The Bible talks about Jesus being crucified since the foundation of the world (see Revelation 13:8, 1 Peter 1:20). This is a concept I can't begin to understand, but what I do grasp is that everything in my past was dealt with by Jesus even before time began. What Jesus did was enough for all of mankind for all time. His representation as God has been present throughout history, and we can look to the Old Testament and see numerous representations of Jesus before he was actually born on the earth. So Jesus has been everywhere for all time and has already paid for every wrong done by me or to me.

Thinking about this also brings to mind a most valuable ministry called Sozo. Sozo was developed by Dawn DeSilva and Teresa Liebscher. Dawna & Teresa are the founders and co-leaders of the International Healing and Deliverance Ministry at Bethel Church in Redding, CA. *Sozo* is a Greek word that means saved, healed, and delivered; and it encompasses restoration of the entire person – spiritually, physically and emotionally. Sozo sessions offer a tool called "Presenting Jesus" that operates on the truth that Jesus has been everywhere for all eternity working on our behalf. The result of using this tool is mind-blowing. I like the Sozo ministry tools because they're effective in pointing people to Jesus, Who has taken care of what any of us are facing.

Let me refer back to the scene between John and Mary. Suppose I'm sitting down with Mary in a Sozo session. The first thing I do, using the "Presenting Jesus" tool, is guide her to ask God this question: "God, is there a memory I need to face that's evoking fear?" God then brings the memory to mind.

Next, I ask Mary to picture herself in that memory, no matter how painful it is. Once she's in that memory, I ask her to look around in it and tell me where she sees Jesus. Based on my past experience with Sozo, I know that the person nearly always finds Jesus—and that he or she is usually shocked that He's there.

Then I ask Mary to focus on Jesus and ask Him this question: "Jesus, what lie did I start believing because of this memory?" Jesus might tell her, "That you aren't valuable enough to stay faithful for."

I then ask her to focus on Jesus and ask Him the next question: "Jesus, what is the truth?"

The possible answers are limitless, but Mary will most likely hear Jesus say something along the lines of, "You are my most valuable creation. I will always be faithful to you. You are loved and adored beyond measure."

And as we pull out of this memory, I simply ask Mary to declare the truth. In that short conversation, something deep happens in Mary that I did not force or conjure. The "Presenting Jesus" tool has allowed her to take one huge step closer to freedom from fear.

The work of Jesus was meant to be applied to every area of our lives—past, present, and future. Many of us believe in the power of Jesus enough for salvation, but not enough for living an abundant life. However, what you believe Jesus did for you is essential to how you'll be able to move on from your past. We've discussed what we believe numerous times so far in this book, but this is one practical activation of belief in our lives.

What you believe will manifest in you. If you believe you have to struggle to earn every ounce of freedom by doing some sort of penance or good works, then that's how you'll live your life. But if you believe that Jesus's sacrifice already purchased every ounce of freedom, then you can rest in the reality that His power heals your every wound and removes your every fear. God is that good.

Some of our greatest wounds are caused by others' choices, not our own. Since God is not a God who controls what people do, the consequences of others' choices ripple throughout the lives of those around them. Sometimes those ripples hit us. The most important thing to remember when suffering because of others' choices is that God didn't cause that pain or that devastating circumstance. On the contrary, He can take the horrendous and miraculously use it for good in your life (see Romans 8:28). God works so closely with the bad in our lives, turning it into good, that a lot of times He gets blamed for causing the bad.

Even the most terrible diseases, wars, and personal atrocities occurred from an accumulation of bad choices throughout the centuries, affecting our air, our food, our bodies, our political systems, our countries, and our personal lives. The real mistake, however, is to believe that God isn't big enough to transform, redeem, and heal in the midst of these painful realities. This belief may be hard to swallow right now, but I encourage you to begin to see God through the lens of the only word in the Bible that identifies His personhood: Love. God *is* Love (see 1 John 4:8). He may have many attributes and characteristics, but He *is* only one thing: Love. What does love look like?

God Is Love, and Perfect Love Casts Out Fear

This beautiful verse, which comes soon after 1 John 4:8, tells us:

> There is no fear in love [dread does not exist],
> but full-grown (complete, perfect) love turns fear
> out of doors and expels every trace of terror! For
> fear brings with it the thought of punishment,
> and [so] he who is afraid has not reached the full
> maturity of love [is not yet grown into love's
> complete perfection]. (1 John 4:18, Amplified
> Bible)

If fear still has a presence in our lives, it's because we haven't allowed love to complete its work on us. The complete work was done by Jesus, past tense, but unfortunately we have the ability at any time to build a dam in our minds that will prevent the flow of love from positively impacting all areas of our lives.

Again, it's Jesus we must rely on to tear down these dams. I want to refer back to my Sozo meeting with Mary to explain "The Wall," another tool where I've seen the power of Jesus at work. Again, if Mary seems to hit a roadblock and isn't hearing the voice of God anymore, it's probably because she and I have hit a wall in her life.

So I ask Mary to ask Jesus this question, "Jesus, is there a wall in my life?" Most likely, He answers, "Yes." At this point, I ask her to ask Jesus, "Is it safe to take down this wall?" If Jesus says "Yes," then we ask Him to show us the wall. Most people then see something physical, like a fortress, a chain-link fence, or a wall in their home. I then ask Mary to ask Jesus, "Do You have a tool to give me to take down this wall?" The answers again could be limitless, but let's say He gives her a pickaxe. At this point, I give Mary permission to take down the wall with the tool, and Jesus usually joins in on the process.

Now, these Sozo processes are not formulas you must follow; they simply affirm and represent the power of what Jesus already accomplished. It's no surprise that in both "Presenting Jesus" and "The Wall," it's Jesus Who does the work, provides the tools, and applies the healing. This is exactly what happened at the cross where Jesus gave His life. Many times, the primary role in our own healing is simply to believe that what Jesus did was enough. Both "Presenting Jesus" and "The Wall" are tools I regularly use. I encourage you to begin your own conversations with God. He'll always bring you to the healing person of Jesus, His Son, so He can apply the finished work of what He did to every area of your past. It doesn't have to look like either of these Sozo tools, but I promise you will be led to the finished work of what Jesus already accomplished to overcome your past.

Know Yourself

You would be surprised at how many of us are so swept up into the daily grind that we never really address these questions, much less try to answer them:

- What's possible for me?
- What am I capable of?
- What are my strengths?
- Who does God say I am?
- Who do I say I am?
- Am I an introvert or an extrovert?
- Am I an administrator or a connector?
- What are my passions?
- What are my dreams?

Just as we all do, I know the answer to "What happened to me?" But I can't move past "What happened to me?" without knowing who I am. Otherwise, I'll continue to allow what happened to me to define who I am.

Now, I'm all for personality tests and strengths assessments, but I think that knowing you're a child of God is even more powerful than knowing the results of those tests and assessments. Each and every one of us was created in His image, and those who believe in Him have the power of God radiating within them. These two facts alone make victory over any area of our lives possible, regardless of what tests and assessments tell us. The foundation of knowing ourselves is to understand what it means to be a child of God. Explore His heart, listen to His voice, and allow others to speak His words over you.

One way to align yourself with who He says you are is to make declarations. We talked about this much earlier, but now I want to take declarations to the next level. About three years ago, I attended a worship school where Dan McCollam led an amazing session that had an instrumental impact on me. Dan McCollam has trained thousands of believers around the world to write original songs of praise and worship using their own ethnic sounds, styles, languages, and instruments. Dan is the director of Mission School of Worship, a once-a-month training school in Vacaville, CA. Dan guided our group through a session that empowered us to move from just believing in the good things God says about us to declaring them as our identity. We were asked to look over all the powerful promises and words we had received over our lives to create a list of "I am" statements.

I started by reviewing all the prophetic words in my life, by rehearsing the promises that God had given me through scripture, and by combing my journals for what God had said to me in private. Then I wrote a list focusing on who I am:

- I'm a leader.
- I'm a songwriter.
- I'm a prophet.

- I'm an overcomer.
- I'm a lover of God's heart.

I then began declaring these over myself daily. It was amazing that after a few weeks, I felt significantly strengthened. I began to believe what God said, and in turn I no longer felt like a victim of my past. I knew that my past was no longer what defined me.

Know Your Strengths and Weaknesses

Despite what I just said about personality tests and strengths assessments, I still do find value in them because I believe that one of the most beautiful and powerful gifts God has given us is our individuality. We were all meant to shine a unique aspect of God's glory that only we can shine. Without each one of us shining our own unique light, the world is missing something. That's why in 1 Corinthians 12, the Apostle Paul speaks of the body of believers as all being unique and necessary separate parts. The body would be of no use if we were all acting as a foot or a hand. We need all the parts of our body if we're to function as we were meant to.

So many of us think, "If I could be more like so-and-so, then I wouldn't struggle so much with the things I do," or "If I could be more like so-and-so, then I'd attain my destiny." But maybe—just maybe—the reason we're still struggling is precisely *because* we're trying to be like that other person. Maybe our destiny feels out of reach *because* we're patterning it after someone else's.

Remember our previous discussion of how God speaks uniquely and individually to each one of us. Throughout the Bible, He uses unique and different means to speak to each and every one of His children. Why? Because He understands our individuality.

He created us, and He loves and celebrates our differences. He wants you to be your first-best you—not a second-best someone else.

When I take the time to understand how I am unique and different, and I move to a place of love and acceptance of my individuality, I can then grow *past* what happened to me and grow *into* who I was created to be. I can also safely surround myself with others who are different from me because I know I need their strengths to complement my weaknesses.

My marriage is a perfect example of this. Rick and I could not be more opposite. I'm introverted, disciplined, diligent, and driven. He's extroverted, relaxed, sensitive, and patient. When we were first married, this used to frustrate me. But we're now at a place in our lives where we share responsibilities in everything. We both homeschool our kids. We both lead a local church. We both administrate a ministry school. And we both run a community nonprofit. We even preach together! We do all of these things as a team. Today, I am so very thankful for our differences. I've come to embrace who he is and, even more, who I am. I have the opportunity to see up close how two different personalities can complement each other to get a job done. He enjoys the people; I enjoy the paperwork. He is high grace; I am high justice. He is the visionary; I am the entrepreneur. He is the one who makes sure we rest; I am the one who makes sure we work.

A couple of years ago, I read Tom Rath's book, *StrengthsFinder 2.0*.[1] It offers a long series of assessment questions that identify your five top strengths. You also receive a detailed write-up that's perfectly tailored to fit your individuality. I learned that my five strengths, which are God-given, are: self-assurance, strategy, relating, belief, and significance. In understanding more about

---

[1] Tom Rath, StrengthsFinder 2.0, (Gallup Press, 2007)

how God created me, I learn where to invest in myself. I don't invest in my weaknesses, but in my strengths.

I'll say more about this in the last chapter, but here I want to state briefly that investing in our strengths is a way of thanking God for who we are. We are who we were created to be. This is the time to embrace your beautiful self, inside and out. This embracing will help you weed out things that are unhealthy for you. This embracing will help you make choices that are more in line with how you were created. This embracing will help you partner with the right people to propel you forward. This embracing will wash away your past and excite you about your future.

You may be thinking that this all sounds too positive or too self-focused. May I remind you that Jesus believed in you enough to die for you. God loved you enough to create you. The Holy Spirit values you enough to empower you. You are worth the attention.

Emotional Intelligence

Included within ourselves are our emotions. Oh, the joy of our emotions. Our past would not even be a problem if we didn't have emotions, right? According to emotional intelligence expert Travis Bradberry:

> The daily challenge of dealing effectively with emotions is critical to the human condition because our brains are hard-wired to give emotions the upper hand. Here's how it works: everything you see, smell, hear, taste and touch travels through your body in the form of electric signals. These signals pass from cell to cell until they reach their ultimate destination, your brain. They enter your brain at the base near the spinal cord, but must

travel to your frontal lobe (behind your forehead) before reaching the place where rational, logical thinking takes place. The trouble is, they pass through your limbic system along the way—the place where emotions are produced. This journey ensures you experience things emotionally before your reason can kick into gear.[2]

In Chapter Two I discussed this idea in relation to fear and how our amygdala works by creating involuntary responses. But if many of our emotional responses are triggered from our past experiences, how do we integrate the journeys we've been on with a healthy emotional life today? One answer lies in something we all possess—the emotional intelligence that Bradberry refers to. Emotional intelligence is defined as the ability to monitor one's own and other people's emotions, to discriminate between different emotions and label them appropriately, and to use emotional information to guide thinking and behavior. Emotional intelligence is made up of four competencies: self-awareness, self-management, social aware-ness, and relationship management.

In the late 1980s, psychologists Peter Salovey and John D. Mayer became the first and leading researchers to focus on emotional intelligence. Here is some of their wisdom on the subject:

If you have high emotional intelligence you are able to recognize your own emotional state and the emotional states of others, and engage with people in a way that draws them to you. You can use this understanding of emotions to relate better to other

---

[2] Travis Bradberry, *Emotional Intelligence 2.0*, (TalentSmart; Har/Dol En edition, June 13, 2009), Kindle Edition.

people, form healthier relationships, achieve greater success at work, and lead a more fulfilling life.[3]

What's most fascinating about emotional intelligence, also referred to as EQ, is that it's the most powerful predictor of success in life. It was once believed that IQ (intelligence quotient) was the best predictor of life success, but that has changed because of various revealing studies regarding EQ. As Travis Bradberry states:

> When emotional intelligence was first discovered, it served as the missing link in a peculiar finding: people with the highest levels of intelligence (IQ) outperform those with average IQs just 20 percent of the time, while people with average IQs outperform those with high IQs 70 percent of the time. This anomaly threw a massive wrench into what many people had always assumed was the source of success—IQ. Scientists realized there must be another variable that explained success above and beyond one's IQ, and years of research and countless studies pointed to emotional intelligence (EQ) as the critical factor.[4]

It's often not the smartest people who are the most successful or the most fulfilled in life. You probably know people who are academically brilliant and yet socially inept and unsuccessful at work or in their personal relationships. On its own, a high IQ isn't enough to guarantee success in life. Yes, your IQ can help

[3] Peter Salovey & John D. Mayer, "Key Skills for Raising Emotional Intelligence," *Helpguide.org*, February 2015, http://www.helpguide.org/articles/emotional-health/emotional-intelligence-eq.htm.

[4] Travis Bradberry, *Emotional Intelligence 2.0*, (TalentSmart; Har/Dol En edition, June 13, 2009), Kindle Edition.

you get into college, but it's your EQ that will help you manage your stress and emotions when facing your final exams. As psychologist Cary Cherniss noted in his study on emotional intelligence:

> At L'Oreal, sales agents selected on the basis of certain emotional competencies significantly outsold salespeople selected using the company's old selection procedure. On an annual basis, salespeople selected on the basis of emotional competence sold $91,370 more than other salespeople did, for a net revenue increase of $2,558,360. Salespeople selected on the basis of emotional competence also had 63% less turnover during the first year than those selected in the typical way.[5]

> For 515 senior executives analyzed by the search firm Egon Zehnder International, those who were primarily strong in emotional intelligence were more likely to succeed than those who were strongest in either relevant previous experience or IQ. In other words, emotional intelligence was a better predictor of success than either relevant previous experience or high IQ. More specifically, the executive was high in emotional intelligence in 74 percent of the successes and only in 24 percent of the failures. The study included executives in Latin America, Germany, and Japan, and the results were almost identical in all three cultures.[6]

---

5 Cary Cherniss, Ph.D., "The Business of Caring for Emotional Intelligence," Consortium for Research on Emotional Intelligence in Organizations, 1999, http://www.eiconsortium.org/reports/business_case_for_ei.html.
[6] Ibid.

Have you ever been given advice like: "Feelings aren't important." "Emotions get in the way." "Don't trust your feelings." "Don't feel sad." "Just trust God." I suspect you have, because many Christians have a serious misunderstanding about emotions in the Christian life. They think Christians should live austere existences and overcome any strong emotions.

Did God have emotions? Did Jesus have emotions?

Jesus's emotions are referred to in the Bible. "You have loved righteousness and hated wickedness; therefore God, your God, has anointed you with the oil of gladness beyond your companions." (Hebrews 1:9) Jesus was happy. But not only that, He felt the whole range of human emotions. He wept over the death of His friend, Lazarus. He sweated blood over giving His life. He felt anger when the temple was being abused. Did you know that the Bible describes more than twenty different emotions that Jesus felt? Jesus felt affection, anguish, anger, compassion, distress, grief, gladness, indignation, joy, love, peace, sadness, sympathy, uneasiness, and weariness. If Christ is our model of perfect spiritual and emotional maturity, perhaps we can learn emotional intelligence by taking a look at a few of His emotions.

How about going all the way back to Genesis to examine the emotions of God? Over and over again in the account of the Creation, all throughout Genesis 1, God saw that "it was good." Goodness is subjective and can only be measured by how one feels about something. As God examined His creation, He felt the goodness it contained. He felt good, and it was good.

But there is no greater example of feeling than God's love. It was that very love that moved Him to give us Jesus. It was the feeling of desire for relationship with us that moved him to develop a plan of reconciliation. Our God feels deeply. His feelings even move Him. And if we go back to our study on the Fear of the Lord in Chapter Three, Proverbs 9:10 implies that getting in touch with what moves God is the beginning of wisdom. So we should not be ashamed of our own emotions. We simply need to learn to manage them.

We can all develop and strengthen our EQ. This is important in dealing with fear because a healthy EQ allows us to examine our past without being overcome. A healthy EQ even enables to more proactively enter into relationships with others without the fear of what is in their past. I'm working on that process myself right now. Let's take a moment and examine the four competencies of EQ so we can identify where we may need growth.

SELF-AWARENESS

In self-awareness, we recognize our own emotions and how they affect our thoughts and behavior. We know our strengths and weaknesses and have self-confidence. I've already addressed this pretty thoroughly in the "Know Yourself" section of this chapter, so re-read some of those strategies. Self-awareness is a foundational key to moving beyond the fear of your negative past.

SELF-MANAGEMENT

In self-management, we're able to control impulsive feelings and behaviors. We're able to manage our emotions in healthy ways. We take initiative, follow through on commitments, and adapt to changing circumstances. How many of us regularly bail on a commitment when we don't "feel" like it? How many of us feel tossed around by what we feel? Many of us are faced with situations that create emotions we don't feel we can endure. I've conducted a lot of counseling in my life, and one of the most powerful lessons I learned in working with others is to never make a permanent decision based on a temporary emotion:

"No temptation has overtaken you that is not common to man. God is faithful, and He will not let you be tempted beyond your ability, but with the temptation He will also provide the way of escape, that you may be able to endure it." (1 Corinthians 10:13)

Good self-management equips us to process the emotions that come with facing our negative past. This is also paramount in overcoming fear.

SOCIAL AWARENESS

Social awareness is the ability to understand the emotions, needs, and concerns of other people. We're able to pick up on emotional cues, feel comfortable socially, and recognize the power dynamics in a group or organization. Jesus stayed in constant communication with His Father. Jesus did and said only what He heard His Father doing and saying (see John 5:19). His Father was in tune with the hearts and minds of every individual in the world. So by following His Father's lead, Jesus could operate out of an awareness of those around Him. We can't be truly emotionally aware of others if we're building perceptions based on assumptions. We have to find out what's in God's heart for others. Social awareness removes the fear of what may lie in others' pasts.

RELATIONSHIP MANAGEMENT

Relationship management is the ability to develop and maintain good relationships. We can communicate clearly. We inspire and influence others. We work well on teams and manage conflict in healthy ways. There's no better example than Jesus, as He was a leader and a servant in every relationship. However, relationship management does not rule out confrontation:

> "Brothers and sisters, if someone is caught in a
> sin, you who live by the Spirit should restore that
> person gently. But watch yourselves, or you also
> may be tempted." (Galatians 6:1).

Although this verse does not speak of judgment or condemnation, it's often misinterpreted toward that bent. The word "restore" in Greek actually means "to raise someone up to who they were meant to be." In healthy relationship management, you and others see the potential in one another and hold each other up to that positive standard. Positive change is not fostered through judgment and fault-finding. We need to fine-tune our ability to see others the way God does.

When we are able to enter into and manage the relationships that come our way, we have the opportunity to 1)learn from others and how they have dealt with their past, and 2)gleam from healthy relationships that will be a strength in helping us overcome our own pasts. Relationship management is another prime tool for eliminating fear.

How Do We Deal with Our Past?

I'm not going to begin to counsel you or teach you about boundaries or tell you how to forgive. There are many other books out there on those subjects. The main thing I want to tell you about dealing with your past is that you should "do something." Don't ignore it. Don't stuff it. Don't rationalize it. Don't try to evade it. If you want to get past it, do something with it. Face it.

I love the way Jesus never dealt with anything passively. He faced every issue in life with aggressive honesty. He was a revealer of truth and allowed the truth of circumstances to do a mighty work. In the book of John, when Jesus came into contact with the woman guilty of adultery who was about to be stoned by zealots, He let the truth be the transforming factor: "Let him who is without sin cast the first stone." (John 8:7) And as the accusers all walked away, one by one, He faced the woman. Knowing well her actions, and despite His knowing, He said, "Neither do I condemn you. Go, and from now on sin no more." (John 8:11) Her lifestyle wasn't hidden. Everything was exposed—out in the open. Despite vulnerably facing her lifestyle choices, Jesus was able to remove condemnation and empower her to change.

When Paul talks about "taking every thought that comes against the knowledge of God captive and punishing it" (2 Corinthians 10:5), this is not a passive recommendation. To take something captive, you have to look at it full on in the face, grab hold of it, and put handcuffs on it. You can't just push it out of your mind or flippantly ignore it and expect your life to have different results. We have to face the things that are still being replayed in our heads. So do something with the things that are still doing something to you. Get counseling. Get a Sozo. Go to a support group. Develop your EQ. Learn more about yourself. Find a mentor. And, most importantly, believe that Jesus dealt with your negative past once and for all. Do something.

REFLECTIONS

In this chapter, we learned that:

1. When our past haunts us, we can take a moment to find Jesus in the memories of our past by using the "Presenting Jesus" or "The Wall" tools. We can ask him to reveal any lies that have been perpetuating fear in us. We can then ask Him to reveal the truth so we can find freedom from the fears of our past that still haunt us.

Spend some time alone with God and ask Him to show you Jesus in the memories of your past. Write down the lies and truths that Jesus reveals.

LIES

_____

_____

_____

_____

_____

_____

TRUTHS

_____

_____

_____

_____

_____

_____

2. It's important to know how God made us, so we can reconcile some of the issues from our past.

Write down at least three strengths that you possess as an individual.

_____

_____

_____

_____

_____

_____

3. Growing in emotional intelligence will equip you to better process the emotions from your past.

Of the four emotional intelligence competency areas (self-awareness, self-management, social awareness, and relationship management), which one do you feel is your strongest?

_____

_____

_____

_____

_____

In which one of the four emotional intelligence competency areas do you see the most room for improvement, and what's your first goal for improvement in that area?

_____

_____

_____

_____

_____

CHAPTER NINE

Vulnerability:
Overcoming the Fear of Relationships

As you read the title of this chapter, your first thought may have been that this topic could arouse fear, rather than eliminate it. Although I admit that the word "vulnerability" stirs up some anxiety in me, it no longer causes me to feel fear.

What I want to communicate in this chapter is that eliminating fear is actually synonymous with living in freedom. And to be free, you have to be able to be you. And to be you, you have to be able to be vulnerable. So, whether we like it or not, vulnerability is actually going to take us one step closer to living a life exempt from fear and full of freedom.

I began a new journey with vulnerability several years ago. My husband had been going through a year of his own struggles after turning forty and contemplating a life/career change. I could no longer depend on the one person I had allowed myself to be vulnerable with for the previous twelve years—not because he wouldn't let me, but because he wasn't in a place where he could help me process things emotionally. My need for emotional intimacy and relational connection grew more intense over that year. It was not appropriate for me to expect to expect my husband to be the sole fulfiller of those needs. In this season, I needed to be more of a giver than a taker in our marriage. He needed that from me. Those are some of the sacrifices we make in marriage.

My sacrifice for Rick didn't change the fact that I was developing a growing awareness of a need I hadn't previously known I had. I've always been the introvert, the "give me some time away from all other people so I can feel sane" type of person. I also have some childhood baggage that reinforces that part of my personality. Abandonment, rejection, and fear of being lied to are only the tip of the iceberg. So being vulnerable with people never felt safe because people hurt me. I honestly should have gone into the construction business because apparently I'm stellar at building walls, particularly around myself. I remember as a kid people telling me I walked around with a "death look" that communicated "Stay the hell away from me!" I was always told that I was quiet. I was a hard worker and became self-sufficient at a young age, both of which conveyed to people that I didn't need them. The older I got, and the more pain I experienced, the more I never wanted to need people again. I thought I was the only person in my life I could trust.

Until I made one of the most destructive choices I've ever made. At nineteen, I married a con-artist.

Obviously, I didn't know he was a con-artist. But I ignored every red flag and made the choice to be with this charming man. Three months into our marriage, my grandfather discovered that my new husband was having an affair and probably with more than one woman. At that point, the puzzle pieces began to fit together, and I did some research of my own. I discovered that while we were engaged, he was still married to another woman in another city. He was telling the woman he was cheating on me with that he was in the middle of a divorce. I also learned that he had never been a golf instructor or army ranger as he had claimed. He didn't only con me, but also my family. My grand-father, my dad's dad in South Texas, had hired him to work in his ministry. But before long my grandfather began to uncover the numerous lies and deceits. Soon after we separated, his name and photo showed up on the local newspaper's "Top Ten Most Wanted" list for grand theft auto. Nice, Melissa. Way to protect yourself.

After this devastating experience in my life, not only was my trust in people gone, but I had also lost the ability to trust myself. I had discovered that even my own choices had a lot of power to hurt me. So the walls were built higher, the fortress was strengthened, and my emotions were locked away in a cellar that had no key. I allowed fear to become my safety net in every area. If I felt suspicious about something, I believed it was true. When I met my current and forever husband, Rick, I didn't cry, show tender emotions, or reveal vulnerability. I lived in suspicion of almost everything he did and said. Rick married a girl who was constantly cheating on him—with fear.

Our marriage definitely has had its ups and downs, but over the years his commitment to me allowed the walls to be chipped away. He walked around the walls of my "Jericho" many more than seven times, and because of that, I was finally able to communicate and grow relationally. As powerful and healthy as that was, he was still the only person I let "see" me.

To get back to what I began recounting at the start of this chapter, Rick was working through his own emotional baggage, and I had become unnervingly aware of my need to reach out to others. One day, I was sent a video of a TED talk by Brené Brown titled "The Power of Vulnerability." It wrecked me... in a good way. She stripped away the myths of shame. She annihilated the masks we all wear. She communicated the power of stepping into something that brings you freedom to truly be you, with nothing to hide, whether people like it or not. She invited you—she invited *me*—into vulnerability.

Something in me broke open during those twenty minutes. After that video, I timidly began to reach out to five different people in my life for strength. I needed their strength. Who, me? I'd always been the one who had held it all together for everyone else in my life. What did this mean, that I needed someone else's strength? I didn't know at the time, but this is a spiritual truth for all of us.

We have strengths that others need, and they have strengths that we need. And we're missing out on the complete picture of the thousand-piece puzzle of life if we don't allow ourselves to fit together in that way. These five friends began to see a "me" in a way that I had never shown anyone as a minister. They saw my fears. They heard my struggles. They witnessed my weaknesses. They walked through my mistakes and destructive choices with me. Some of them even got hurt by me in the process. Vulnerability is messy, but it's real. And who wants to live any other way but real?

The wonderful miracle was that all five of those people told me, "I like this Melissa better." That shocked me. I truly thought I had gone too far, that I had told them too much, that I had left myself too exposed. I thought I might even lose my job as a minister for being too vulnerable. But I was wrong. They liked the vulnerable Melissa. They could relate to her because they felt she could relate to them. They appreciated the fact that I stopped pretending to act as if I had it all together. They were actually strengthened by my vulnerability because it gave them the strength to face their own issues. Beautiful—truly beautiful.

Finding the Right Balance

Warning: There's a pendulum swing that occurs when you step into vulnerability with others for the first time. You can go too far, but being in touch with your motives for being vulnerable will help you to find the right balance.

Don't be vulnerable just for vulnerability's sake. The goal is not to vomit every thought and feeling onto every man, woman, and child just because you can. The goal of vulnerability is freedom —to live as the real you. We share the areas of our life that need exposure to the light. When we hide things about ourselves, they essentially stay in darkness. Nothing can be dealt with until it's seen. And we're the ones who have the power to bring what's within ourselves into the light. Only when something is brought into the light can it receive the nutrients it needs: for growth, for healing, for change —for you.

Examine that mountain you keep circling around—the mountain that creates fear every time you look at it, the mountain in your life that you're not sure how it got there or what caused it to grow so big, the mountain you think no one else can see.

Here are some truths that will help you destroy that mountain:

- That mountain is only a part of something you are experiencing; it is not you.
- That mountain does not define you; it only reveals a crack in the foundation where dirt got pushed to the surface.
- That mountain is not your identity.

Here's another truth: The mountain itself was not created by your actual behavior. The behavior of addiction, for example, is only a symptom of the actual soil on that mountain. The behavior of anger is only a symptom of the actual soil on that mountain. The behavior of manipulation is only a symptom of the actual soil on that mountain. Behavior is what's growing on the mountain, but it isn't the soil the mountain is made of. Whenever we misdiagnose something, we will end up mis-treating it. Then our cures become based on the symptoms instead of the root. Eventually the cure becomes the next pro-blem and the cycle continues. So let's stop focusing on the symptoms and examine the mountain itself. What possibly caused it to grow?

- A lack of self-worth
- The need for approval
- The fear of rejection
- A feeling of disconnection from God and others
- The loss of a loved one
- Wrong beliefs about God
- And other possible deep-seated issues

This list is where our vulnerability begins. Everyone around us already sees what's growing on our mountain: the symptoms of anger, or addiction, or fill-in-the-blank behavior. It's time to get real about the cause, the soil—the mountain itself. And we're the only ones who can do that.

If your mountain has developed from a lack of self-worth, bring that to the light and get ready to be amazed at the love that will surround you. If fear of rejection created your mountain, bring that to the light and watch relationships begin to flourish and grow again. Light dispels the darkness. And vulnerability is what allows the light to do its work. It's not a striving process, just revelation brought to the light.

Why Religion Is the Greatest Enemy of Vulnerability

Religion is the greatest enemy of vulnerability. Now when I speak of religion, I am not referring to any one specific practiced religion, such as Christianity, Buddhism, etc. I am referring to a religious way of thinking, one that emphasizes superiority over others and utilizes fear and control as its primary tools of motivation. I'm speaking of a religious mindset that the

Pharisees and Sadducees of Jesus' day represented. Religion, in this form, is the strongest self-protection mechanism that exists because it allows people to hide behind ritualistic practices. But self-protection kills vulnerability and hinders connection. Religion tells us that our performance gives us value. Religion orders us to follow rules to be righteous. Religion says we must appear holy to be holy. Religion says that messiness is not godliness and that it will keep you out of connection—with religion.

My husband, Rick, likes to say that he is a "recovering Pharisee" because he used to hide his weaknesses behind the guise of religion. As long as he was reading his Bible, coming to church, and teaching Sunday school, his past addiction to pornography could stay hidden. As long as his mentors and pastors had a positive view of him, he could keep his low self-worth hidden— under the radar.

I, unfortunately, am a recovering Pharisee as well. My critical views of others' faults have allowed me to ignore my own. My socially acceptable coping mechanisms of being a workaholic and perfectionist allowed me to judge others and stay comfortably self-righteous. It's much easier to stay in an unhealthy state of being when your coping mechanisms are more socially acceptable than those of other people. Being a hard worker looks a lot better to the outside world than a porn addiction. But hard work didn't mean I was healthy. I was just able to live in hiding much longer than Rick could, and that wasn't a good thing. My masks needed to come off.

My Encounter with a Real God

Nothing will teach you the art of true vulnerability like a real encounter with God. I mentioned earlier that I have in a ministry called Sozo (the Greek word for "saved, healed, and delivered)," but I also work in another ministry called *Shabar* (the Greek word for "broken-hearted or shattered"). These two ministries are inner healing ministries where, in sessions with individuals, together we ask God to bring to light what He wants to deal with during each session. I learned very quickly that God isn't afraid of vulnerability or the messes in people's lives. He'll bring everything right to the surface.

On one occasion when I was in a group Shabar training, we watched a live Shabar session with a young woman. This particular girl had experienced intense abuse and pain from others. God brought this directly to the light to be dealt with. She was guided to ask God the question, "God, what do you think of these people who have brought me abuse and pain?" She listened and then replied, "God says He thinks they're being assholes." The entire room gasped and then giggled silently. You could feel the religious mindsets in the room being prodded with a hot iron, including my own. What?! God curses?! I have to tell you, I got another level of freedom from religious thinking that day. When I witnessed that God is more concerned about healing brokenness than He is with keeping a "clean mouth," it changed me. God wants us to be real before Him and others, to be as we are so He can help us live as who He made us to be. During that session, I realized that in some ways I was still hiding behind my religious mask, so I wouldn't have to deal with what seemed "unclean" to me.

The truth is, God already calls us clean, even before everything appears cleaned up. God sees us as He sees Jesus. And, in turn, He has no fear in helping us face our messes because He knows that the ultimate clean-up job was already performed for us long ago by Jesus.

Religion only creates more fear. It creates a fear that says if you behave unacceptably, you're unacceptable. Being unacceptable results in disconnection and rejection. So in religion, we hide. Who wants to be honest if they might get cut out . . . or cut up? My guess is that if you've been raised in any kind of religious circle, you have a bit of fear about being truly vulnerable, especially with authority or father/mother figures. This is saddening and a deception. God is a father first. He's a father who loves you unconditionally and celebrates you whole-heartedly.

One of my favorite stories in the Bible is the "prodigal son" in Luke 15:11-32. This was a son who ran off and squandered the inheritance his father had given him. He destroyed his life by making one bad choice after another until he ended up living in filth and misery. At rock bottom, he finally decided to head home because he knew even if he had to live as a servant in his father's home, he would be better off than he was.

But he wasn't a servant. He was a son, and when he returned, his father's response was the clincher of the story. His father threw a party—the richest, most elaborate party—for his prodigal son. Why? Because his son had returned to the place where he would rediscover his true identity. His father offered nothing but complete forgiveness and love. And that changed the son. It wasn't punishment, brashness, or ridicule that shook this prodigal son back to reality. It was the kindness of his father.

Each and every one of us has this Father. He's here right now, looking at you with eyes of compassion and reaching for you with a heart of relentless love. Religion, in its deceptive and controlling form, has told you the opposite. Religion has perverted God into a monster that you must obey or else. Through the lens of religion, God comes across more like a raging, alcoholic father. Religion has not brought us closer to righteousness—it has kept from knowing the One Who is Righteous. The One who made all things right... for you, for me, for all of us.

Vulnerability and the Need for Control

When we feel fear, we want to control things because we only fear what we can't control. This type of religion I have been criticizing can be a cunning tool of control because it looks so holy and appears so godly. In reality, this is a lie.

Control is not love.

I've come to believe that the saying "God is in control" is derived from that type of "religious" thinking. True love does not control. True love allows us the freedom to choose. If God controlled us into loving Him, would it really be love that we were giving Him? He wants us to *choose* love. Freedom is His love language to us. Do you like being controlled? Does it make you feel loved when someone tries to control you or your life? The answer to these questions is most likely "no." Then why have we mislabeled our loving God as a God of control?

I love the scene from the movie *Evan Almighty* where God says to Evan's wife, "God gives opportunities. If you pray for patience, do you think God is just going to make you patient? Or is He going to give you the opportunity to learn patience?" God isn't controlling us into our character. He's giving us opportunities to take risks, to make choices, and even to fail. And then He also gives us the opportunity to be vulnerable about it. We have opportunities every day to learn and grow, because we have a God who so lovingly gave us the freedom to do so.

Religion only takes your freedom away, which inevitably breeds more of one thing: fear.

My Friends and Me

One of the five friends I mentioned at the beginning of this chapter once said to me, "Melissa, I think you have a lot of appointments but not many friends." Ouch. She was right. My busyness made it possible for me to keep my nice, secure mask on. But if I actually took the time to just be—to just be me with other people—how would that change my life?

I'll tell you how, because I've now taken off that mask. I no longer live in fear of shame. Being honest and open about my victories and struggles has allowed me to experience love from others that does not have conditions. I'm more comfortable in my own skin. I actually see the real me even more clearly than I did before—and I like her.

A lack of vulnerability comes not only from our fear of others seeing us but also from our fear of truly facing ourselves. But once we face ourselves, the journey becomes an adventure. And when we bring others into our adventure, life becomes a great ride.

One day, God gave me such a powerful revelation from the book of Matthew that I'll never look at it the same way again. I was spending time in His presence when I suddenly began to see a vision in my mind of the following scripture: "Enter by the narrow gate. For the gate is wide and the way is easy that leads to destruction, and those who enter by it are many. For the gate is narrow and the way is hard that leads to life, and those who find it are few." (Matthew 7:13-14)

I envisioned two roads, both the same size and same width. I saw myself on the first road, all alone. The road felt so wide. But it only felt wide because I was the only one on it. It was a path of isolation and independence. Then the vision transitioned, and I saw myself on the second road. It was full of people. Trying to walk down this road was like trying squeeze through a crowd in a concert. It felt narrow and tight. I then heard God say, "The narrow road is narrow because it requires doing life with people, relationships, and trust. On the narrow road, you'll bump up against and squeeze past a lot of people. The wide road is wide because it's the one people choose to travel all alone. But it abandons the concept of interdependence and loving others."

I was so deeply impacted by this vision that I went straight to the scriptures looking for confirmation. Interestingly enough, most translations of Matthew 7:13-14 add a topic break—a subheading added by the translators—between verses 12 and 13. According to the translators, verse 13 begins a new thought, which is about the gates. But those subheadings were never in the original manuscript. The scriptures in the two verses are meant to be one continuous thought. Verse 12 says, "So whatever you wish that others would do to you, do also to them, for this is the Law and the Prophets." Wow! I clearly saw the confirmation I was looking for. Verse 12 is saying to "Do unto others as you would have them do unto you," and then verse 13 says to "Enter through the narrow gate." The two verses coming together, one following the other, enforce a theme of relationship and interdependence.

It was during those minutes with God that I finally felt compelled to venture into being the vulnerable person God meant me to be. My excuses for labeling myself as "the introvert" or "not a people person" had been removed. I clearly realized that I do indeed need people.

I would later come to find out that people needed me, too.

Vulnerability in Our Church

This movement of vulnerability in my life started a ripple effect in our church. I've never experienced "family" within church walls as I have with the group of people at The Church at

Parkview. I began to be more real with my struggles and fears from the pulpit, and in response to that vulnerability, others came forward searching for the same freedom. Our leadership began to see the need to foster honesty regardless of the consequences and in turn offered grace-filled solutions that ensured hope and victory.

For the past ten years, our motto as a church has been: "Real people. Real questions. Real answers." How can I expect anyone else to be real if I'm not? And so I continue this journey of vulnerability. Will you join me?

REFLECTIONS

In this chapter, we have learned that:

1. Vulnerability creates an opportunity to get to the root causes of our struggles.

Write down some areas of your life where you need to be more open and vulnerable.

_____

_____

_____

_____

_____

_____

2. Religion tries to convince us that vulnerability isn't safe, but it's actually trying to keep us from rising to our greatness as children of a loving Father.

Create a list of people you feel led to reach out to, and begin a journey of vulnerability. Think of someone who could be a spiritual mother or father.

_____

_____

_____

_____

_____

_____

3. God isn't afraid of our struggles. He'll stay right with us and assist in cleaning up our messes.

Spend some time alone with God and ask Him to show you how you can begin cleaning up certain relationships.

_____

_____

_____

_____

_____

_____

CHAPTER TEN

Preparing for the Worst:
Dealing with the Fear of the Unknown

Fear is a thief. It stole walking on the water from Peter, and surely it stole
from the other eleven disciples as well.
Bill Johnson

Late one evening in the summer of 2005, our family was coming
home from a night out together. We pulled up to our three-
bedroom, two-story townhouse in Southern California, and were
all getting out of our van to go inside when we heard a voice
yelling in panic and realized it was aimed at us. Rick and I turned
around to see that our neighbor had pulled up at the end of our
driveway. She was leaning out the window and screaming, "A
tsunami is coming! Head to higher ground!" Then she peeled
away leaving us looking at each other in bewilderment at what
just transpired.

Rick shrugged and continued into our home—but I froze… in
fear. A tsunami was coming! We needed to leave! I begged Rick
to get our family out of the area and to higher ground. He tried
to reassure me that everything was fine. There were no sirens.
No one was else was fleeing. We were fine.

But I wouldn't hear of it. I felt sick with anxiety and fear. Rick
finally gave in, and we drove about two miles to our friends'
home to see what they thought. We turned on the television

news, watched the reports, and finally decided it was safe for us to stay in our homes.

I felt silly for flying into such a panic, but the feelings had been reality for me, regardless of what reality actually was.

The feeling of fear dictates the choices made for many others as well, as shown in a 2014 National Institute of Mental Health survey of Americans' fears and worries[1]:

FEAR AND WORRY STATISTICS	DATA
Percent of things feared that will never take place	60 %
Percent of things feared that happened in the past and can't be changed	30 %
Percent of things feared that are considered to be insignificant issues	90 %
Percent of things feared in relation to health that will not happen	88 %
Number of Americans who have a diagnosed phobia	6.3 Million

In addition, the survey listed the top ten phobias in the US population as[2]:

---

[1] National Institute of Mental Health, "Fear/Phobia Statistics," Statistic Brain, July 8, 2014.
[2] Ibid.

	Top Phobias	Percent of US Population
1	Fear of public speaking – Glossophobia	74 %
2	Fear of death – Necrophobia	68 %
3	Fear of spiders – Arachnophobia	30.5 %
4	Fear of darkness – Achluophobia, Scotophobia or Myctophobia	11 %
5	Fear of heights – Acrophobia	10 %
6	Fear of people or social situations – Sociophobia	7.9 %
7	Fear of flying – Aerophobia	6.5 %
8	Fear of confined spaces – Claustrophobia	2.5 %
9	Fear of open spaces – Agoraphobia	2.2 %
10	Fear of thunder and lightning – Brontophobia	2 %

Fear is a real emotion even when what we fear isn't real. When we allow fear control over our lives, we begin to shrink away from truly living. Or, at a minimum, we settle for a different kind of living.

A good example would be "extreme preppers." Preppers are people who believe that a catastrophic disaster or emergency is likely to occur in the future and who make active preparations for it, typically by stockpiling food, ammunition, and other supplies. However, extreme preppers are usually operating out of fears rooted in conspiracy theories rather than realistic preparedness.

The prepping community has grown exponentially in the wake of such recent disasters as the 2010 Haiti earthquake, the 2010 Deepwater Horizon oil spill, and the 2011 Tohoku earthquake and tsunami. Although wisdom is always the tool we want to utilize for our decision-making, many times extreme preppers do not. Instead, fear is the guiding force behind many of their decisions while trying to cope with extreme anxiety about the next looming calamity.

When extreme prepping becomes the obsessive lifestyle of individuals, it proves that they have little to no trust in a God who will protect, prepare, and provide. Some extreme preppers even have an element of fear in their relationship with God because they believe He's the one who sends such calamities. Ironically, think about the fact that insurance companies call natural disasters, "Acts of God." And we wonder why many people, like some extreme preppers, still carry some fear in their view of God. God gets blamed once again.

There is, of course, some justification to being prepared for life's unexpected twists and turns. We should save. We should be wise. We should invest. We should practice prevention. These are all wise actions to take. But when do we cross the line from wisdom into fear?

The Age of Twenty-Seven

I used to be afraid I was going to die at the age of twenty-seven. I can't explain it. It wasn't rational. There was no good reasoning behind it. No one in my family had died at that age.

Still, at some point years before, I heard this thought in my head, "You're going to die at twenty-seven." So my twenty-seventh year of life was rough. I didn't want to do anything that could possibly be even remotely dangerous. No driving up mountains. No flying. No going into the ocean. I know, it was ridiculous, but in my mind…it was real.

At that time in my life, I didn't know that God doesn't speak in fear, so I couldn't identify the source of that thought. I still believed that God allowed bad things to happen as part of His will. I didn't trust Him completely. I didn't have the tools or revelation and knowledge I have now, so my thought became a declaration, which became a belief, which affected my behavior.

I was recently reminded of what I had gone through at age twenty-seven while reading this discussion of "the complexity of fear" and its effects on decision making by psychologist Maria C. Lamia:

> There is another important aspect of emotions to consider that, in the case of fear, may be important to decision-making as well as survival. That is, when an emotion is triggered, it has an impact on our judgments and choices in situations. In a study of risk taking, participants who were fearful consistently made judgments and choices that were relatively pessimistic and amplified their perception of risk in a given situation, in contrast to happy or angry participants who were more likely to disregard risk by making relatively optimistic judgments and choices. Similarly, individuals whose traits are fearful—those who tend to have personality characteristics that are dominated by the emotion of fear—will avoid taking risks that are generally perceived by others as relatively benign. Thus, awareness of your emotions and considering how they might influence your

decision-making in a given situation is important in your approach to life, your work, and your goals.[3]

Her comments confirm my earlier statement in Chapter Two that "fear is the paralyzer of healthy decision making." It's no longer just about the decision right in front of you. It becomes about your life, your work, and your goals. Will you live consumed with preparing for the worst in every situation? Or will you live life with hope and faith in a future of possibility?

Whatever you decide will affect today. And tomorrow. And your destiny. This is not a matter to be taken lightly.

Do you wonder why some people can never seem to get ahead in life? Why as soon as some people get up, they fall back down? Why it seems that there's a magnet in their lives that's attracting negative circumstances? Maybe this is even you.

In the simplest of terms, negative people attract negative circumstances. A blanket statement like that may not seem fair to say, but it's been proven both scientifically and biblically. And this brings us back around to examining our belief systems, our thought patterns, and our emotions, because these develop the core of who we become.

If your version of reality is negative, you're conditioned to believe that whatever can go wrong will go wrong—and that whatever can go right will most likely go wrong too. The beliefs you hold develop you into a negative person without your being aware of it.

---

[3] Maria C. Lamia, "The Complexity of Fear," *Psychology Today*, December 15, 2011, https://www.psychologytoday.com/blog/intense-emotions-and-strong-feelings/201112/the-complexity-fear.

Here's a quick evaluation tool for evaluating how negative we may have become:

- Do you complain? All the time or just some-times?

- Do you often discuss what's wrong in the world more than what's right? This includes the 'ter-rible' weather, 'horrible' traffic, 'idiotic' govern-ment, 'lousy' economy, 'stupid' in-laws, etc.

- Do you criticize? All the time or just with certain people?

- Are you attracted to drama and disaster? (Can you unglue yourself from the TV when there's a news story of a disaster? Can you avoid getting involved in the lives of dysfunctional celebri-ties?)

- Do you blame? All the time or just certain situa-tions?

- Do you believe that you have no control over most of your results?

- Do you feel like a victim? Do you talk about people doing things to you?

- Are you grateful for what is or will you be grateful when things finally start going right for you?

- Do you feel like things are happening to you? Or do you feel that they are happening through you?

If you answered 'yes' to more than half of these questions, you may be looking at life through a negative lens.

I Turned Off the Bad News

I still remember when I stopped watching the news. I was seventeen and living on my own for the first time. I had a nice apartment that I shared with a great roommate. But being on my own made my mind wander to all the scary possibilities of what could happen to me or to us or to our apartment.

My roommate loved watching the news, almost religiously. Every day at 4 p.m., 5 p.m., 10 p.m., and again at 7 a.m. would come the doomsayers and naysayers and stories of horror. At least that was how I perceived the news. Because I was someone who struggled with fear, the news seemed to offer constant confirmations that danger could be headed my way.

So I made a decision. I wasn't going to watch the news anymore. "The news may be fine for others," I decided, "but it's not good for me." One of the wonderful things about living in grace and freedom is that I'm able to make choices and create boundaries for myself because I want to and not because I have to.

We all have the freedom to do anything, but is everything good for you? The news isn't good for me. That doesn't mean I keep my head in the sand. I watch headlines. I read carefully-selected articles online. I'm also married to someone who devours the news, so he keeps me updated. I'm simply creating a healthy boundary for my own mind. I have the same boundary when it comes to scary or gory movies. Others may have no problems with those movies, but they aren't good for me.

I love how the Apostle Paul addresses this subject in the New Testament when he says: "All things are lawful, but not all things are helpful. All things are lawful, but not all things build up." (1 Corinthian 10:23) Anything is allowed, but not everything is going to benefit you. Exercise your will and authority in deciding what those things are for you.

Cultivate the Positivity Inside of You

The Apostles Paul and Peter were both imprisoned separately in the Bible. Both of them were able to sustain themselves with hope, and even joy, in those circumstances. We've heard concentration camp stories from World War II where the survivors were usually those who believed and held on with faith. One inspiring example was American pilot Louis Zamperini, who survived a plane crash that left him stranded on a raft in the Pacific Ocean followed by years in a Japanese prison camp. As told in *Unbroken*, the 2010 book that was followed by a 2014 film about his life, he overcame all the obstacles he faced with resolve, humor, and sheer will.[4]

These survivors tapped into what lies in all of us: Faith. Positivity is simply a result of the powerful faith we discussed in Chapter Four. I won't digress into repeating the teachings on faith, but instead I want to offer five practical solutions for activating faith and turning it into a life of positivity that attracts positive circumstances:

1. SHIFT YOUR THOUGHTS TO THE POSITIVE

When I focus on something I love, I become more loving and more positive. When I focus on something I think is bad, I immediately shift towards the negative. If you focus too much on things you dislike and don't want, you're going to be predominantly negative, so it won't be surprising if you attract predominantly negative experiences and dysfunctional people.

---

[4] Laura Hillenbrand, UNBROKEN: A Story of Survival, Resilience, and Redemption, (New York: Random House, 2010).

2. MAKE DECLARATIONS

Proverbs 18:21 says: "Death and life are in the power of the tongue." To see life flourish, we must manage our words. Your words create your world. God spoke creation into existence. Review the first half of this book to remind yourself the power of your words in your life.

3. FOSTER GOOD PHYSICAL HEALTH

Our physical well-being has a strong influence on our thoughts and emotions. If you're out of shape and keep eating food you know isn't healthy for you, it's more difficult to attract the right circumstances into your life because you'll feel unhealthy and undesirable.

When I'm taking care of my body, I personally feel a difference in my ability to have self-control over my emotions and actions. My mind is clearer. My energy is higher. My attitude is healthier. So I'm naturally more positive.

4. DEVELOP HEALTHY BOUNDARIES

Don't take on other people's stuff or serve as an emotional "garbage can." Don't endlessly give your energy to others without getting anything in return. Don't feel so sorry for others or take on too much responsibility in misguided attempts to help them.

Establishing and maintaining healthy boundaries means knowing and setting your limits in life. For example, because we live in a parsonage on the church property, we can potentially be bombarded with drop-by visitors at any time of the day or night. But my introverted personality can't handle that. So when we have people over, I kick them out, gently, of course, at 9:00 p.m.

Also, when people knock on the door, I don't answer if I'm busy, and I open the door just a crack if I'm not. I'm protecting the boundary of my home.

Resentment is a negative emotion. And resentment usually grows from feeling taken advantage of or unappreciated. But these issues will only occur if people are unaware of what taking advantage or being unappreciative of you looks like. It's our job to communicate these things. People value you by valuing your boundaries. You value yourself by creating them. It has been said by life coach and author, Tony Gaskins, "You teach people how to treat you by what you allow, what you stop, and what you reinforce." Setting boundaries teaches people to treat you with respect.

5. SET DESTINY GOALS.

Having healthy beliefs is the key to moving our lives in a positive direction. Outlining goals that help renew the way you think is highly effective. Imagining a positive future is a crucial aspect of positive thinking. So spend some time pondering:

- What are your dreams?
- What has God put in your heart?
- What have people told you you're called to?
- What excites you?
- What moves you to tears of passion?

Now ask yourself what steps you can take to move toward those things. This isn't a "striving" exercise. This is an "ask God to show you, and write it down" exercise. It will help stir up what He has already placed in you. Just as water and sun make seeds grow, start feeding the seeds inside you—and watch your life flourish.

The World Must Be Coming to an End

In the fall of 2014, the world found itself in the midst of a crisis called Ebola. A virus that kills more than 60 percent of its victims, Ebola was spreading on some continents, but primarily in Africa and West Africa. The first cases in the United States occurred in late September 2014, and over the next two months a total of only ten cases were recorded in the United States.

But when that first case hit US soil, panic struck the nation like nothing I'd ever seen. The media blew everything out of proportion. Health officials were estimating that we would see more than 150 cases by the end of the year. Many people I knew were making preparations as if an apocalypse was imminent. People's terror that they had somehow contracted the disease began causing irrational behavior.

I became even more interested in the whole epidemic when I began coming across articles by observers like risk perception and communication consultant, David Ropeik, who argued that the fear of Ebola would cause more illness than Ebola itself:

> Ebola is starting to pose a serious risk to public health in America. But the threat is not the disease itself. The real danger is a growing epidemic of fear, an infection that spreads much more readily than the virus, is far harder to treat, and which threatens to cause much more sickness and death. The longer this epidemic of fear persists, the greater the likelihood that fear of Ebola in the United States will harm public health far more than the deadly hemorrhagic virus itself.

> As entertainingly explained by Robert Sapolsky in his wonderful book *Why Zebras Don't Get Ulcers*, chronic stress increases blood pressure and raises the risk of cardiovascular problems, the leading

cause of death in America. It depresses our immune system, which means we are the more vulnerable to catching infectious diseases, or more likely to get sicker from them, or die from them, than we otherwise would be. It is highly likely that fear of Ebola will cause more people to get, or suffer more from, influenza, which the CDC says kills between 3,000 and 49,000 people per year.

Chronic stress depresses fertility, bone growth, memory, and healthy digestion. And it interferes with neurotransmitters associated with mood, increasing the likelihood and severity of clinical depression. Suicide is the 10th leading cause of death in America.[5]

Over the centuries, the world has experienced many pandemic tragedies, from "natural disasters" to swine flu to economic recessions—and all of them have taken their greatest toll through the avenue of fear.

Why? Because fear sells. Fear sells medicine. Fear sells stockpiled supplies. Fear sells healthcare. Fear sells more fear, which sells more stuff.

I'm honestly not a conspiracy theorist, and I keep my nose out of politics 95 percent of the time. But I can look around and come to a quick conclusion that fear has an effect not only on American health but also on the American economy. You can decide whether that effect is good or bad.

---

[5] David Ropeik, "Fear of Ebola. A Greater Risk Than the Disease Itself," *Big Think*, October 2014, http://bigthink.com/risk-reason-and-reality/criticism-of-ebola-mistakes-in-dallas-puts-us-at-greater-risk-than-the-disease-itself.

Let's Make a Difference

The most beautiful part of eliminating fear from your own life is that you're not only making a positive impact on your destiny—you're also making a positive impact on the destinies of others around you. And those destinies will have a positive impact on those around them and so on and so on until our city, country, and world are positively impacted. America was founded on the principle of freedom, but today fear has become the new foundation on which many Americans base their lives. By eliminating fear from our lives, we are rebuilding the foundation of freedom.

This obviously translates spiritually as well. Freedom was won for everyone in existence on the cross when Jesus gave his life. Freedom is the place where we learn how to grow in faith and be perfected in love. Fear is an enemy to those concepts. Let's take back the freedom that's rightly ours by eliminating fear from our lives:

- No more fear of God.
- No more fear of life.
- No more fear of tragedy.
- No more fear of other people.
- No more fear of Ebola.

- NO MORE FEAR OF FEAR.

REFLECTIONS

In this chapter, we learned that:

1. Fear is a real feeling that works to counteract positive movement in our lives.

Take a moment to write down three areas that you have negative thoughts about.

1.

_____

2.

_____

3.

_____

Now write three declarations that will help turn your thoughts positively towards those areas.

1.

_____

2.

_____

3.

_____

2. The fear of tragedy is many times worse than the tragedy itself. It keeps us from the freedom that has already been won for us.

Spend some time with God and ask Him to show you your life in complete freedom. He may give you a vision or a word of hope. Write that down.

_____

_____

_____

_____

_____

CHAPTER ELEVEN

It's Too Good to Be True: Enjoying Life Without a Fear of Enjoying Life

A few years ago, I was in the Bahamas staying at the famous Atlantis resort when something very interesting happened. I was sitting inside the resort's cigar shop, The Havana Humidor, with Rick and my father. I was smoking one of their brand-name cigars (yes, I enjoy an occasional cigar) when I suddenly noticed something strange. I looked down at my cigar and saw what looked like fine glitter covering the cigar. I would liken it to what gold dust must look like. I examined it closely. I certainly didn't remember seeing it when I had started smoking the cigar. I grabbed Rick's cigar and examined it…nothing. I grabbed my dad's cigar and examined it…nothing. I hurried to the back of the humidor room to check the box of cigars mine had come from…nothing. This phenomenon was only occurring on my cigar!

At that moment, I could feel the presence of God very strongly. It hit me. This was something supernatural. But why? I sat back down on the couch, closed my eyes, and began a conversation with God in my head. I felt Him reminding me that He gave us this world to enjoy. I began seeing images of tobacco use centuries ago, when it was used as an analgesic and for peace offerings, and then fast-forwarding to the moment the tobacco was creating for me now.

The Pleasures We Were Created For

Okay, time out.

Have I freaked you out? Where the heck am I going with all of this? Am I about to condone smoking, drinking, drugs, and more? Here's my quick answer: no. And here's my complicated answer: yes—but only for what God intended.

Please take a deep breath and stay with me. I promise you I'm not a heretic.

I want to start with some verses from the Bible about the goodness and pleasure in life that God intends for us to enjoy:

> "How precious is Your lovingkindness, O God! Therefore the children of men put their trust under the shadow of Your wings. They are abundantly satisfied with the fullness of Your house, and You give them drink from the river of Your pleasures. For with You is the fountain of life; in Your light we see light." (Psalm 36:7-9, New King James Version)

> "You will show me the path of life; in Your presence is fullness of joy; at Your right hand are pleasures forevermore." (Psalm 16:11, NKJV)

> "But seek the kingdom of God, and all these things shall be added to you. Do not fear, little flock, for it is your Father's good pleasure to give you the kingdom." (Luke 12:31-32, NKJV)

"He loves righteousness and justice; the earth is full of the goodness of the LORD." (Psalm 33:5, NKJV)

"You crown the year with Your goodness, and Your paths drip with abundance." (Psalm 65:11, NKJV)

"For by Him all things were created: things in heaven and on earth, visible and invisible, whether thrones or powers or rulers or authorities; all things were created by Him and for Him. He is before all things, and in Him all things hold together." (Colossians 1:16-17, NKJV)

Let's start with that last verse in Colossians. God created all things, and all things are held together and sustained by Jesus, in heaven and on earth. Is it possible that many of the things God created to bring us pleasure have been stolen and perverted into destructive versions? And is it possible that the perversions of all we were meant to enjoy have caused us to throw out the original version that He intended for us? If so, the originals have been thrown out because of our fear of indulging in the perversions.

Jesus said He came to give us life and life abundantly (see John 10:10). I believe there are pleasures and experiences that God meant for us to enjoy, but we aren't enjoying them because of our fear of the perverted versions.

It's time to eradicate the fear of pleasure and realize we carry within us the DNA of God, who loves pleasure. It's in our nature to desire and long for pleasure. Those around us need to know that in God and in His creation is found every pleasure imaginable. It's possible that the reason others don't know this is because we, who believe in God, do not find our pleasure in God ourselves, so we can't display the beautiful examples of what can be enjoyed in Him. Many of us have avoided pleasure ourselves. Or when we haven't avoided it, we've secretly settled for the perversions instead.

These are very important concepts to ponder because the world is hungry for God. Our society seems to be longing for the miraculous—for the supernatural, for the sensual, for mind-altering states. You can see it in the popularity of vampire and zombie movies. You can see it in the massive growth of the pornography industry. You can see it in the fascination with magicians, horoscopes, and psychics. You can see it in practices like Reiki healing. People are longing for the transcendent experience that can only be fully satisfied in God. I would even venture to say that most Christians are still longing for the same thing as well.

The Graycliff Wine Cellar

My strange experiences in the Bahamas didn't stop after the cigar. God was teaching me something and shaping a new belief in me that permanently altered my life. During that trip, my father, Rick, and I all took a trip to the cigar factory where Graycliff cigars are made. They are hand-rolled with precision and excellence. It's a beautiful process to watch.

Aside from the cigars, the Graycliff property also has a wine cellar with more than 100,000 bottles of wines dating back to nearly a century. This wine cellar is underneath the cigar factory. The manager took us on a private tour and began to explain the vintages of the wines we were seeing. The history behind many of these wines and the sheer artistry of how they had been created began to overwhelm me. As we walked into the tasting room where they bring dignitaries and celebrities to taste some of their best bottles, I began to feel a sense of being drunk. I hadn't had one single drop of alcohol that day. But the presence of God became so thick to me in that tasting room that I saw a haze of light fill the air, and I was physically overcome. The beauty of what His children had created in that cellar was so intoxicating in and of itself that I felt drunk on the creative force behind the creation of the wine. I didn't even need to drink the wine to feel it. I'll never forget that moment. Even now, writing this book, I can feel that moment flooding back to my being.

What does this mean? I want to answer this question while proposing some possibilities that we could be missing out on— and examining some of the perversions that have become substitutes for what God meant for us to enjoy.

DRUNKENNESS

Let's start with drunkenness. I love a good beer or a great glass of wine, but I don't believe that using these substances to the point of intoxication is ever healthy or leads to a good outcome. I do believe, however, that our desire to *feel* drunk is natural and even validated by the Bible: "And do not get drunk with wine, for that is debauchery, but be filled with the Spirit." (Ephesians 5:18) The parallelism in this verse reveals that the feelings of both are similar but come from two very different sources. So, we can enjoy God's creation of alcohol in moderation while experiencing our intoxication in life from the Creator: "I am like a drunken man, like a man overcome by wine, because of the LORD and because of His holy words." (Jeremiah 23:9b)

Many times in God's presence have left me feeling "drunk." And since God is with me all the time, that can happen pretty often. But for an example, one of the clearest experiences in my mind and one I've always remembered was when I was healed of megacolon. As I was receiving prayer to be healed of megacolon, I toppled over sideways on the pew with such heaviness that it was as if I was drunk. I felt wonderful, full, and warm inside, and I could feel the presence of God enveloping me. It was in that moment that I received healing.

GETTING HIGH

Since we started with drunkenness, we might as well continue with getting high.

Drugs create mind-altered states, but drugs are only a perversion of the real thing. I believe that visions, dreams, and experiencing the heavenly realms are the mind-altered states God meant for us to enjoy, as the Apostle Paul described:

> "I must go on boasting. Though there is nothing to be gained by it, I will go on to visions and revelations of the Lord. I know a man in Christ who fourteen years ago was caught up to the third heaven—whether in the body or out of the body I do not know, God knows. And I know that this man was caught up into paradise—whether in the body or out of the body I do not know, God knows—and he heard things that cannot be told, which man may not utter." (2 Corinthians 12:1-4)

In this verse, Paul is actually talking about himself. He recounts his own story in vague terms so as not to freak anyone out, but he still needs everyone to know. This is not the only "out of body" experience found in the Bible. Peter, too, had a vision that changed the course of Christianity (see Acts 10:9-16). Also, Ezekiel in the Old Testament refers to being taken to physical locations "in the Spirit" numerous times. (see Ezekiel 11 and Ezekiel 43) And in Acts 8:39 the Apostle Philip was physically relocated by the Spirit of God from the water where he was baptizing the eunuch to (the town of Azotus. All of these were mind-altering encounters.

I myself have had many similar experiences that I would liken to Peter's and Ezekiel's. I often see visions that God uses to speak to me about my own life or about another's. And without fail, when I trust these visions, amazing things happen. A clear example would be when I had a vision of three different winds coming to bless a friend's life. Over the next few months, my friend experienced a physical, an emotional, and a spiritual shift in his life that he likened to three separate winds of God working in His life.

Regarding my similarities to Ezekiel, many times when I'm hanging out praying to or worshiping God, I will suddenly see myself in a foreign country. In my mind's eye, I'll begin to follow God's lead. I'll ask Him where I am and what He wants me to do. One day, for example, I saw myself in China. Physically, I was still in the midst of a worship service at church, but spiritually, I was in China ministering to a young Chinese girl and her family. I felt that her home would be used for a Bible study and that her home and family would be catalysts for the underground church coming above ground. While I was ministering there in the spirit, I suddenly became aware of the worship service I was in again—and I heard the person leading the worship service saying, "I feel like we need to pray for China. We need to pray that the underground church becomes the above-ground church." I opened my eyes in shock and disbelief. God had just completely confirmed my mind-altering experience.

SMOKING

Did you know that nicotine actually has health benefits? It's an awful substance to inhale into your body. But when used properly, nicotine actually reduces the chance of Alzheimer's disease and is even being explored as a treatment for diabetes. So why is it that we, as a culture, so often decide to use nicotine improperly? If you've ever smoked a cigarette, you've experienced the overwhelming calm that permeates your bloodstream and makes you feel relaxed—or, might I say, at peace. Peace is something we were created to experience.

Philippians even says we should be experiencing a peace that surpasses all understanding! "And the peace of God, which surpasses all understanding, will guard your hearts and your minds in Christ Jesus." (Philippians 4:7)

God is the source of the peace we're all searching for, but nicotine has been used as an inferior substitution. Philippians 4:6, reminds us that simply taking all our requests to God will release that peace. Let's redeem nicotine for its positive uses instead of trying to obtain peace with it. And let's discover satiating peace in God.

SORCERY AND WITCHCRAFT

God gave us the mind of Christ and the keys to His kingdom. With those gifts comes an ability to see into the future and to see into the hearts of mankind. Romans 12 and 1 Corinthians 12 mention many gifts that employ these abilities, including prophecy (the ability to speak into someone's destiny or future); word of knowledge (to know something about someone revealed to you by God); and word of wisdom (to apply the revelation of God into the life of another).

All of these gifts require a connection to God, which we all have! Many hunger and thirst for this connection they don't realize they have, so perversions like sorcery, witchcraft, horoscopes, tarot card reading, palm reading, and psychic encounters have risen to the surface to satisfy our desires. People all over the world are experiencing the supernatural, but their lives are suffering because those experiences aren't coming from God. We're meant to see into the future with the eyes of God and to use what He shows us to prophesy and encourage those around us, but many have avoided that completely out of the fear of falling into the perversions.

LUST, PORNOGRAPHY, AND PROSTITUTION

It sounds oversimplified to say that we were all created for love, but the truth of this becomes clear when we can see so many people hungry for love. Love is in our DNA, as God is love Himself. When we don't experience the giving and receiving of love, we'll look for substitutes. People will abuse others' bodies to meet their need for love, even if only through pleasure and only for a moment. That is why more than 27 million people are being held captive in sex trafficking rings around the globe today, and why pornography has grown into a multi-billion-dollar industry. Results of studies are now being released on how pornography negatively affects our brains. The drive of lust can feel like a great substitute for love, but in the end it leads people into destructive addictions.

Instead, let's demonstrate real love to everyone we meet. How will anyone know about the abundance of goodness found in the love of our God if we demonstrate only hate, indifference, or judgment? As Romans 2:4 says, it's the goodness of God that leads people to change. His goodness is most greatly displayed in His love. That's what people truly desire.

DEPENDENCE ON MEDICATIONS

I want to be very careful about how I approach this subject because I do believe that God uses many avenues to heal, including medications. What I do want to ask, though, is, "In our time of need, do we turn first to God, or to our medicine?" Every time I have a headache, you'd better believe I'm going to pray before I think about taking a painkiller. And then I'm going to ask Rick to pray. And then I'm going to ask my kids to pray. And only after that might I take a painkiller. Again, medications certainly are necessary in many situations, but have they replaced our belief in the healing power of God?

Healing is another gift given to us by God. Why? Because He wants us to experience pleasure. Because He's a God of abundant life. Because He's a God of redemption. I myself have been healed of megacolon, and I've seen people healed of diabetes, cancer, carpel tunnel syndrome, and minor headaches. Don't settle for a pill until you've first gone after the source of healing in God.

CELEBRITY

"Celebrityism" is what I actually call it. There is such fascination with celebrities in our world, especially here in the United States. Whether sports celebrities, movie and TV celebrities, money-making celebrities, or fifteen-minutes-of-fame celebrities, many of them get more attention from us than our own loved ones do. We study them. We research them. We follow them. We want to be like them, know them, and dream about them. But why?

I believe that we were all created with a longing to follow. It's called discipleship. Jesus' last command before leaving earth was, "Go and make disciples." (see Matthew 28:19) A disciple is a follower. A disciple is someone who models his or her life after another. We're meant to follow. We're meant to model our life after another: Jesus. But when we don't accept His example to look up to and His standard to emulate, we replace Him with another. We want to be inspired, encouraged, and challenged by the lives of those around us. We were created that way . But celebrityism has become our modern-day perverted version of discipleship.

AND I COULD GO ON...

Yes, I could go on, because the perversions above only scratch the surface, and one day I may write a book on this subject alone. There are so many other perverted versions and replacements out there... Humanism for faith. Demeaning comedy for joy and laughter. Gossip for encouragement. Think of any one thing that is supposed to bring pleasure in our life with God, and you can probably find a perversion that's developed to keep us from truly finding pleasure in the original.

Pleasure Is Found in God

It's time to reclaim and redeem the encounters that God has dreamed for us. We're talking about the almighty God of the universe. When He encounters this small, human body, the only thing I can imagine I would experience is something supernatural. Let's not allow our fear of what we haven't yet experienced in Him keep us from experiencing Him. It's always a danger to create a belief system based on lack of experience. For example, if I haven't experienced the goodness of God in an area, that doesn't give me the right to say He isn't good.

The mindset we have to confront is, "What do I believe is possible with God?" I've met people who have found gemstones lying around. I haven't experienced that myself, but do I believe it's possible with God? I've heard testimonies of people who have been dead for two weeks coming back to life. I haven't experienced that either, but do I believe it's possible with God? I have friends who have seen a limb on someone else's body grow out that wasn't there before. I haven't experienced that, but do I believe it's possible with God? I've listened to stories from people who have levitated, been transported, and have had a cloud of gold dust around them. I haven't experienced those things, but do I believe they are possible with God? Yes, I believe in all these things and more, even though I have not experienced them.

Many times we get so caught up in our skepticism that we don't stop to consider our actual belief system. Many times the belief we're facing is whether we believe God can do something or not.

Let's say that someone is lying about his or her testimony. I still stop to ask myself, do I believe that God could do it? Even if a person didn't get raised from the dead two weeks after he or she died, is that something I believe God could do? Yes, I do.

I've been on many "trips" to heaven. I've gone to various countries in the spirit. I've seen angels. I've been drunk and high in God's presence. I've been hit with a holy laughter that went on for almost an hour. I've twitched under the power of God. I've seen people healed with my own hands. I've prophesied over hundreds of people. If you haven't experienced some or any of these things, the question isn't whether I'm telling the truth or not. The question is, do you believe that these things are possible with God?

Is It Too Good to Be True?

If you're not enjoying your life, have you left God out? God designed us for pleasure, and He designed pleasure for us. I hope you believe that God wants us to enjoy life in Him. It's the lack of belief in this truth that has perpetuated the common fear that when life is going well, it means "life is too good" and even that "something bad must be about to happen." Most of us have been there and can relate. But that fear is derived from several twisted beliefs:

- That God is out to get us or even punish us.
- That I'm not worthy enough to experience this much happiness.
- That life is supposed to be hard.

The truth, though, is that while trials and tribulations inevitably come our way, the true difficulties are not the circumstances themselves but how we choose to respond to them. If we believe we're destined for misery, then our joy will continually be robbed. But if we believe that God will redeem all things for our good (see Romans 8:28), then we'll live with a fullness of joy and hope. Let's take our focus off the negative and place it on everything that God has for us to enjoy.

Enjoying God's Creation

God is good. So we can look around at our world and say that everything He has created was meant for good. Right?

I'm not sure we actually feel that way, though. I think many people believe that when we become followers of God, certain elements of this world become taboo. We can no longer reap the benefits of His world out of fear that we might abuse them. I have a news flash—anything can be abused. The Bible can be abused. The Bible has been used for slavery, power, and control. The gifts of the Spirit can be abused. I've the seen those gifts used for manipulation, domination, and intimidation. Our relationship with God can be abused. Many have used their intimacy with God as foundation for pride. But even our abuse of all these wonderful things doesn't stop God from giving them to us. God isn't afraid of our choices or even our abuses. If He was, He wouldn't have put two trees in the garden in the book of Genesis.

Here are a few examples of the things in this world that we're meant to enjoy without abusing them:

- Food without gluttony
- Alcohol without drunkenness
- Tobacco without addiction
- Sex without lust consumption
- Money without loving it
- The earth without worshipping it

Every one of the items in this short, and by no means exhaustive, list has a richness of value. They're all kisses from a good God who wants to give us good gifts.

God's desire is for us to experience pleasure is in the utterly decadent display of His goodness. He is so good. Even when the circumstances around us deal us a bad hand, God can win with a pair of twos.

I love the story in Exodus 33 when Moses goes up the mountain to commune with God and boldly asks Him to show him His glory. God replies, "I will make all My goodness pass before you, and I will proclaim the name of the Lord before you." (Exodus 33:19) God's glory is revealed in His goodness. How wonderful for us! To experience the glory of God is to experience every good thing He has in store for us.

This leads me to ponder this verse: "For the earth will be filled with the knowledge of the glory of the Lord as the waters cover the sea." (Habakkuk 2:14) It doesn't say that the earth will be filled with the glory of the Lord. It says that the earth will be filled with the *knowledge* of the glory of the Lord. For the earth to know His glory, someone has to be teaching it, displaying it, representing it—and that's us! As Romans 8:19 says: "For all creation waits with eager longing for the revealing of the sons of God."

The earth is waiting to hear from us. We must display His goodness around us. To do that, we have to experience His goodness first.

Enjoy God

The last perversion, which I've left out of this chapter so far, is the clincher for me: Religion is a perversion of relationship. Author and international speaker, John Crowder, defines religion in this way, "Religion is trying to get what you already have." God is here…with you. Relationship with Him is always on the table, but religion has told us that it is something we have to work to acquire. It's just another perversion. We are designed for relationship with Him. And in that relationship is every pleasure imaginable.

I have to go back to one of my favorite verses: "You make known to me the path of life; in Your presence there is fullness of joy; at Your right hand are pleasures forevermore." (Psalm 16:11) While His creation is enjoyable and His gifts are enjoyable and the life He gave me is enjoyable, still nothing compares to the joy of Him. In His presence is *fullness* of joy. This life is meant to be enjoyed because you sit at the right hand of God. It's not too good to be true.

Take a moment today, even just five minutes, and ask God these questions:

- "God, what do you think of me?"
- "God, what do you have for me?"
- "God, what do you want me to enjoy?"

I think you'll be surprised by the answers. Maybe you'll even have your own confirmations while enjoying life in the Bahamas.

REFLECTIONS

In this chapter, we learned that:

1. God created us for pleasure but many perversions have developed to divert us from the pleasure found in Him.

Write down at least three areas where you've substituted perversions of pleasure for the pleasures of God.

_____

_____

_____

_____

_____

2. God created this world for us to enjoy.

Write down things in this world that you want to see redeemed for God's glory and for our pleasure.

_____

_____

_____

_____

_____

_____

3. God wants us to enjoy Him.

Spend some time alone with God and allow Him to show you the pleasures He has for you. Allow Him to wipe away your fears. Take notes.

_____

_____

_____

_____

_____

_____

CHAPTER TWELVE

The Culture of Investment:
Investing in Yourself and Others

When Rick asked me to marry him on January 20, 2001, a new fear struck me like none other that I had ever known. It was a fear familiar to many people, which I call "the fear of commitment." Some people claim this fear as an excuse to never get married, to not ever take on a responsible job, or to never have children. But the issue lies much deeper than a surface fear. It isn't a fear of commitment—it's a fear of risk.

After having experienced some abandonment as a child, infidelity in my first marriage, and abuse in other relationships, the idea of committing to another person for the rest of my life aroused a trepidation in me that was hard to shake. The commitment was not necessarily the issue as much as the level of risk I saw in front of me. I kept asking myself: "What if it doesn't work out? What if I get hurt? What if I love him more than he loves me? What if I'm not good enough? What if I fail?"

I loved Rick deeply and I was thrilled at the idea of us getting married, but my fear of the risk involved was something I had to face before I could fully commit. I had to make a choice to invest.

Investment.

The word sounds simple enough, but it's charged with so much depth and meaning. Investment is what makes companies run, marriages thrive, churches flourish, and bank accounts increase. Investment is an all-in choice to stay and commit in the face of risk. Amazingly, I've discovered that investment is also an antidote to fear. It laughs in the face of worry and anxiety and takes control of the situation. Investment is a manifestation of faith.

Let's start by looking at some of the dictionary definitions of "invest"[1]:

> **1:** to commit (money) in order to earn a financial return
> **2:** to make use of for future benefits or advantages <*invested* her time wisely>
> **3:** to involve or engage especially emotionally <were deeply *invested* in their children's lives>

In looking at these three definitions of "invest," I see three potential areas for fear: finances, the future, and vulnerability. (I've already addressed one of these, vulnerability, in Chapter Nine.)

When I think of someone who invests, certain types of people come to mind:

- A *farmer* invests hard work into the land, invests money to pay laborers and buy seed, and invests time to care for and grow.

- A *collector* invests by paying a high price for the most valuable item.

- A *financial investor* takes a risk on something that might fail because he believes in it.

---

[1] http://www.merriam-webster.com/dictionary/invest.

What I deem respectable about these people is their ability and willingness to use the combination of their time and resources to take a risk. The farmer's crops may fail. The collector's collection may decrease in value. The investor's stock may plummet. But all of them take risks. As I said in Chapter Four when talking about faith and fear, faith is actually spelled R-I-S-K.

If faith is spelled R-I-S-K, then investment, which is always a risk, is actually a huge step of faith. Whether it's a financial investment, an investment in a relationship, or an investment of time and energy, you're exercising your faith. You're stretching it to the next level.

Let's do a breakdown of the three definitions of "invest" and see how developing a "culture of investment" within ourselves can affect our lives and free us from fear. I'm going to work backward with the definitions of "invest" and start with number three.

"Invest" Definition 3: "To Involve or Engage, Especially Emotionally"

This goes back to our chapter on vulnerability. When you commit to engage in an emotional relationship with another person, the risk is always high because we're human, and humans make mistakes. The potential for gain, on the other hand, is even higher.

I have a best friend, Jeni, who has stood with me through thick and thin for over twenty-five years. We met in fourth grade, when I was nine years old. I didn't like her. She was popular. I wasn't. I kept her at an arm's length (or longer) at all times. Then, suddenly, in fifth grade, she began reaching out to me. I didn't know what to think or how to take that. I honestly was frightened by the idea of her friendship. We were very different. I had a broken home. She didn't. She was beautiful and blond. I was the brunette who hadn't quite grown into her own yet. I already had glasses. She didn't. She had older parents who were settled and stable. My family wasn't in that place. And I had just been diagnosed with the rare and serious disorder of megacolon.

But there I was, a frightened, insecure ten-year-old girl who decided to take the risk of investing in this friendship. Today I can say that Jeni and I have been through everything together. And it turned out that I was actually the more dangerous one to be in a relationship with. I hurt her and even turned my back on her more than once. But she never abandoned our friendship. She stayed committed to me, and her parents did as well. She's been forgiving, loving, and more generous than many other people in my life. She is my best friend to this day.

It wasn't always easy. It took work. We had fights. There were times when I didn't think our friendship would survive. But we chose to invest, and we're still reaping the benefits. She's one of the main reasons I can still believe in people. She has taught me about goodness and hope. Her parents have been a rock for me. I can't imagine the life I might have had if I had allowed the "fear of Jeni" to dictate my decision in fifth grade. I would be missing out on a lot.

Aside from friendships, marriage is probably the best example of emotional investment that requires great risk but has an even greater payoff when you choose to invest. Aside from the fact that I had not grown up with great role models in marriage, my husband, Rick, had an addiction to pornography early in our marriage that cost him a lot. It was an unfortunate and very real experience that we had to process. But I was determined not to allow this experience to build a negative belief in my life, so I chose to continue to invest in my marriage and in my husband regardless. I haven't been the easiest person to stay committed to either—a woman fighting against fear can be an unstable woman at times. But Rick has chosen to continue to invest as well, in himself and in us.

Rick and I have both chosen "investment" as a core value in our marriage. Once or twice a year, we go to a conference or read a book that's helpful to our marriage. We've instituted a weekly time to discuss difficult issues, which forces us to stay vulnerable and open. We also hold tightly to a weekly date night. On top of that, when we reach times that make either of us want to quit, we see a counselor. Our marriage has been the epitome of investment.

I can say that I love Rick today more than ever. I can say that our life is moving in the best direction it ever has. And I can also say that our relationship is the healthiest it has ever been emotionally, spiritually, and sexually. Is it because we've suddenly got it all figured out? No. Rick still encounters temptation. I still face fear and control. But we've both chosen to invest in ourselves and each other to grow as individuals and as a couple.

Speaking of investing in yourself, this may be your number one most difficult investment to make. Many people are excellent at investing in others but unable to invest in themselves. Psychologists call this codependency. Jesus was wise enough to be aware of this tendency and included a powerful statement about it in what he deemed in the New Testament as one of the two greatest commandments of all time: "Love your neighbor as yourself" (see Matthew 22:36-40). What this basically means is that your neighbor needs for you to love yourself. Your true ability to give affection, attention, and committed investment to others is directly related to your ability to give the same to yourself.

We can't run away from ourselves, so we try to push down all our self-loathing and find our approval in other people. But all this does is suffocate them and turn them away. We need to be people who believe in the greatness that God created in us. We need to believe in the destinies we all carry. We need to believe in who we really are in Him.

God is the greatest encourager I know. I think He knew we would need it. He says that we're no longer servants, but His friends. He calls us His very children with an inheritance to enjoy. He declares that we're royal, holy, righteous, perfect, and brand new in Him. God wants you to believe those things about yourself as much as He does. The more you value yourself, the more your relationships will flourish. Take care of you. You're amazing—and worth the investment.

Choosing a stance of investment, relationally, will plant your will firmly even when swayed by winds of fear. Your commitment to others and to vulnerability will wear down fear's power, and you will find yourself enjoying the benefits of relationships…freely.

"Invest" Definition 2: "To Make Use of for Future Benefits or Advantages"

This aspect of investment can be summed up in one word: stewardship.

When you hear the word "stewardship," you probably think immediately about something financial. But stewardship is actually applicable to your entire life. Stewardship is about increase, not management. Let me remind you of the financial scenario I used in Chapter Seven as an example of this principle: If you're given $100, good stewardship would not be to simply manage the same $100 for the next five years. Good stewardship would be to handle it in a way that brings about an increase.

The culture of investment makes the most sense when you apply it to yourself. Examine yourself:

- What are your strengths?
- What are your gifts?
- What are your positive traits?

- What is noteworthy about your character?

Now . . . what are you doing with those gifts, qualities, and attributes? Are you simply going to manage what you've been gifted with and just fiddle around with some of your strengths from time to time? Or, even worse, are you going to allow your gifts to lie dormant? Instead, become a good steward of what you've been given.

I've always been a naturally good public speaker. This became apparent when I took public speaking in college. The interesting thing is that I was terrified every time I spoke. This could easily have caused me to hide my natural talent and not do anything with it. But the joy and sense of accomplishment I felt at the end of every speech drove me to make a choice to invest in this gift of mine. So I made communications my major and joined the college speech team.

I immediately saw the benefits as my skills increased. I learned new tools and began to overcome my weaknesses. Most people would stop right there, but when I chose to invest, it was a commitment. So what am I doing today? I speak at a local ministry school in front of people on a weekly basis. I preach as one of the ministers at our church on a monthly basis. I teach a high school public speaking class to our countywide homeschool organization, and this requires that I study the textbook regularly. I watch national speeches online, and I continue to write new speeches myself. I also believe that one day I'll speak in front of many more as I continue to invest in what God has given me.

Investment is a forward-motion commitment. You don't just commit to stay in place. You don't commit to stand still. You commit to take a risk with every step you take, and you don't ever stop taking those steps, no matter what fear will try to tell you.

There's a belief in our culture that we should spend more time turning our weaknesses into strengths instead of focusing on our strengths. It's especially prevalent in the education system. When a child shows a lack in an area, time and energy get poured into improving that area. While I understand the principle of developing a well-rounded child, the system fails to nourish or encourage gifts that could grow stronger, because all its investment is being poured into improving weaknesses.

In the fall of 2011, I went to a songwriting workshop in St. Louis called "Write About Jesus." I was in a class taught by musician and worship leader, Carl Cartee, in which he approached this subject from a musical standpoint. He said (and I'm paraphrasing), "Let's say I'm a good rhythm guitarist, but I don't play lead guitar very well. I could spend five hours a day working on my lead guitar skills and maybe on a scale of 1 to 10 improve my skill level from a 3 to a 3.5, whereas if I spent one hour a day working on my rhythm guitar skills, I could improve from a 6 to a 9." As he explained this, I could clearly see the benefit of investing in the gifts God had given me.

Do you realize how valuable your individuality is? Do you really know how precious you are? In the Old Testament, God asked Moses to build a tabernacle to house His presence. God had specific instructions for how this tabernacle was to be built. It was very important to Him. The right amount of precious metals, unique measurements, chosen builders, etc. were involved. It's estimated that the tabernacle would have cost approximately $12 billion to construct today.

Fast-forward to the days of King Solomon centuries later. God instructed King Solomon's father, David, to construct a temple to house His presence, which Solomon had the privilege of building. Again, it required very specific instructions, many skilled laborers, and a whole lot of gold. This was also very valuable to God, and it was important how it was built. It's estimated that the temple would have cost approximately $70 billion to construct today!

Fast-forward to now. Where has God chosen to house His presence today? In His children! How valuable must we be? I'm going to guess priceless. In His eyes, we're more valuable than a structure overlaid in pure gold. Yet sometimes we talk about and treat ourselves like mere aluminum, simply because we don't have the same gifts as someone else. We compare our innate talents, qualities, and abilities to those of others – and we downplay who God says we are.

We're all different. We're all meant to be different. We each were created to shine a unique aspect of God's glory that only we can shine. When we don't invest in our unique abilities, the world is missing a glowing characteristic of God that we each, individually, were meant to put on display. It's not a good aspiration to be a "Jack of all trades" because the flip side of that is that you'll end up a "master of none." Be you. Invest in you. Always.

Investment in our future will begin to eliminate the fears that are lying to us about our abilities, our capabilities, and our destinies. Investment is a lifestyle of saying "fear will not dictate my future."

"Invest" Definition 1: To Commit (Money) in Order to Earn a Financial Return

Since the dictionary puts "money" in parentheses, I'm going to say that money can easily be interchangeable with time. Time is money, right? And we all know that the quickest way to discover what your heart values is by examining where you spend your time and money. Next to people in our lives, time and money seem to be our most precious commodities. We hold what we do with those two things very closely. In fact, many people spend time and money hiding what they do with their time and money because time and money provide such a telling picture of a person.

But here's where fear begins to lie to you: "If you give your money to anyone else, you won't have enough for you." "If you spend too much time at church on Sunday, you'll miss football." If...if...if...if...

Money spent on yourself and time for football are both great things. I personally indulge in them both. But when you know you're supposed to be investing elsewhere, suddenly the fear may come that there won't be enough to go around. This is what I call a "poverty mindset." A poverty mindset doesn't just apply to someone who's in financial poverty. A poverty mindset is a lens through which people view life. And it's directly related to fear.

This fascinating article by author, professor, and cofounder of Jensen Learning Corp., Eric Jensen, on "The Effects of Poverty on the Brain" develops this point:

> Many still believe "the poverty problem" is about a lack of money. Unfortunately, it's not that simple. In fact, if that were the only problem, it would be good news, but it's not. Poverty is a chronic, mind/body condition exacerbated by the negative, synergistic effects of multiple, adverse, economic risk factors. The effects of poverty on any human being are truly staggering. In short, the kids are different because their brains are different. Our neurons are designed by nature to reflect their environment, not to "automatically" rise above it. Areas of the brain that are affected by chronic exposure to poverty include those responsible for working memory, impulse regulation, visuospatial, language and cognitive conflict (Noble, et al. 2005). Evidence suggests children of poverty are more

likely to have different brains via four primary types of experiences. They are: 1) exposure to toxins, and 2) chronic stress 3) chronic exposure to substandard cognitive skills and 4) impaired emotional-social relationships.

In sum, we know that children of poverty often have suboptimal brains and we know that brains can change for the better. There are seven primary factors that drive positive change in the human brain. They include novel complex learning, physical activity, *hope*, managed stress levels, and a supportive, *hopeful* social climate. Each factor feeds off of another; hence physical activity lowers stress and the *hope* feeds the academic skill-building. These factors are not new to most educators, but the real challenge comes with collaboration, consensus, *commitment* and *compliance* to use them.[2] (emphases added)

In the last paragraph of this quote, I've emphasized many words that confirm much of what I've talked about throughout this book, obviously *hope*, which is the fuel for *faith*. But how about the need for *commitment* and *compliance* to make a change for the better? This sounds like *investment* to me.

Many of us can identify with one of the four causes of a poverty mindset that Jensen lists—toxins, chronic stress, exposure to substandard cognitive skills, and impaired emotional-social relationships. We begin to build truths for our lives as children, when our brains are still in the formative state. We come to

---

[2] Eric Jensen, "The Effects of Poverty on the Brain," *The Science Network*, 2006, http://thesciencenetwork.org/docs/BrainsRUs/Effetcs%20of%20Poverty_Jensen.pdf.

believe that there is not enough money, not enough food, not enough love, not enough understanding, not enough compassion, and not enough room for us. This idea of "there won't be enough for me" is the foundation of the poverty mindset, which is rooted in fear.

Generosity is impaired in our lives when the threat of not having enough time or money keeps us from making the investments that would actually bring increase into our lives. But there is a storehouse of abundance for us! I do not believe that we have a God Who would ask us to give away and be left wanting. In fact, Jesus said, "Give, and it will be given to you. Good measure, pressed down, shaken together, running over, will be put into your lap. For with the measure you use it will be measured back to you." (Luke 6:38) The very act of investing with generosity activates a spiritual principle that releases more of the abundant life right back to you.

A few years ago, in a vision, I saw a heart with four main ventricles coming out of it. Each ventricle led to an area of my life: ministry, work, family, and spouse. The heart was our money. And I felt God saying to me, "I want you to invest your finances in this way: 25 percent in each ventricle/area of your life." Being self-employed, it made sense to give 25 percent back into my work, which includes my gifts and talents. I also love my kids, and I homeschool them, so I invest a lot of time in them. So I could resolve to invest 25 percent into those three lovelies of mine. And then Rick and myself, individually and as a couple, have always been a huge area of investment, so I felt fine with giving 25 percent there.

But giving away 25 percent of our money back to God was more than just a challenge. It was scary! We did it anyway. That next year, we structured our finances in a very specific way to give our money equally to the four areas, 25 percent each. And not surprisingly, we were more blessed financially that we had ever been. We were blessed with a brand new laptop, a ten-day family missions trip to La Paz, Mexico, and an all-expenses-paid vacation to Puerto Rico. Plus we were able to do more investing in ourselves that year in terms of leadership and ministry-specific training. It was amazing to see God work with our generosity.

I grew up with chronic stress in my life, and I've seen it take its toll on my mind. I used to be afraid of Rick having friends because I thought he wouldn't have any time for me. I used to never want to give money to people in need because in my mind we needed it as much as they did and there wouldn't be enough. I used to never invest my time in hobbies, watching television and things I enjoyed because there wouldn't be enough time for the "important" things in life that would bring me "success." I'm thankful to have moved away from many of those streams of thought.

I want to be a person of generosity. God is. And I know that to be a person of generosity, I have to be willing to invest my time and my money. Period. This heart of investment will not allow fear to have a grip on my life.

How Are We Valuing What We Invest In?

There are three levels at which people make the choice to invest in something:

- Price
- Product
- Purpose

When you choose to invest in something at the *price* level, when the price changes, so does your commitment: "This is costing me too much now. I no longer want to invest in this."

When you choose to invest in something at the *product* level, when the product changes, you abandon ship. Even if the change is positive, your investment was in the product as it used to be: "This isn't the scent that this face soap had when I first bought it." "This position at my work isn't what I originally signed up for." "You aren't the man I first married."

However, when you choose to invest at the *purpose* level, your investment is secure. No matter whether the price or product changes, you're staying invested because you believe in its purpose: "I buy into the philosophy of Apple products." "I work for this company because of their core values." "I believe in the benefits of marriage even as we both grow and change."

Look at the areas of investment in your life where you've found it difficult to keep your commitments. Is it because you only went in only at the price or product level? Has something changed that's now creating fear? Your level of investment has to be on the purpose level. God's investment in you was. He knew that you would change and grow and morph and maybe even break His heart. But His purpose was relationship – and that was worth the ultimate investment.

Investment Eliminates Fear

The culture of investment forces us to face our fears in the midst of risk. As we develop this culture in our lives, fear will begin to dissipate. Fear *only* has the amount of control that you give it. Fear *only* has influence where you allow it. Fear *only* has a voice when you listen.

Investment mocks fear. Investment says "I am. I will. I have."

Investment builds forward motion in your life. Investment sets you up for increase. Investment creates a mindset of security. Investment is an antidote to fear.

REFLECTIONS

In this chapter, we have learned that:

1. Choosing to invest in life will counter the fears of life. Our commitment to risk will inspire courage and hope.

Write down at least three dreams in your life that you want to invest in.

1._____

2._____

3._____

2. Emotional, financial, time, and energy investments combat every fear and engage wisdom as the decision maker for your life.

Write down one way you will invest in each of the dreams above.

Dream #1

_____

_____

_____

Dream #2

_____

_____

_____

Dream #3

_____

_____

_____

CONCLUSION

Wisdom, Faith, Investment

Even as we are all on our own road to freedom from fear, know that freedom has already been won for you. It's been won by a God Who loves you. As we are eliminating any fear we have had of this God or in our relationship with this God, we will discover that our entire lives are being freed from fear in the process.

In addition, you do not have to strive for victory over fear, for Jesus has already defeated fear. He has made you free. Your belief in that truth will bring more freedom than you could ever work for.

Jesus' victory also won you the building blocks for thriving. Wisdom, faith, and investment are the building blocks for the foundation of your new life of freedom. I encourage you to continue to become more aware of who you are, and enjoy the goodness God has for you.

May wisdom become your new compass for life decisions.

May faith become your anchor in the sways of life.

May investment become your mentality as you pursue your destiny.

Fear won't stand a chance.

Melissa Joy Wood is a fourth generation minister with a rich heritage of Christian leadership. Melissa has been a Worship Pastor for seventeen years and a Senior Pastor for nine years alongside her husband, Rick.

Melissa has an education in Communications and Theology that has afforded her the opportunity to be involved in many successful ventures. She and Rick were the Directors of Avenue Revivalist Ministry School in Ventura, CA for 4 years. Melissa has been teaching high school public speaking to homeschoolers in the county for 5 years. Melissa has also been invited to speak in many locations to share her journey and life message.

Melissa and Rick also started a nonprofit in 2013, The Destiny Hub, whose goal is unite faith-based leaders across the county for networking, encouragement, and community transformation. The Destiny Hub has been a catalyst for bridging the local community to faith-based organizations.

Melissa is the mother of three amazing children, Abigail, Brennan, and Caleb. She and Rick homeschool them and love every minute of it.

CPSIA information can be obtained
at www.ICGtesting.com
Printed in the USA
LVOW01s1557191115

463343LV00014B/844/P